Flavors of Lahore: A Collection of 98 Traditional Recipes

The Crispy Crust

Contents

INTRODUCTION

Introduction for cookbook "Flavors of Lahore: A Collection of 98 Traditional Recipes"

Welcome to Flavors of Lahore: A Collection of 98 Traditional Recipes! This cookbook is filled with the wonderful flavors of the city of Lahore, Pakistan, renowned for its rich and flavorful cuisine. It showcases the classic dishes of the area and provides easy-to-follow instructions for creating delicious meals.

Lahore has been called the 'heart of Pakistani cuisine' for good reason. Here, the locals have developed an extensive range of unique and traditional recipes, some of which are featured in our cookbook. Our recipes use wholesome ingredients and authentic flavors to bring the best of Lahore's food culture to your kitchen.

The book features recipes for breakfast, lunch, dinner, snacks, and desserts, all with detailed instructions that assist you in perfectly preparing each dish. Whether you're an expert chef, a novice or a busy parent looking for a quick meal for the family, our book promises to bring a sense of satisfaction to your table. Enjoy a variety of recipes like sajji (barbecued meat), falooda (a sweet drink made with milk and vermicelli), chicken cholay (curried chickpeas with chicken), and desi keema (minced beef dish with potatoes).

Our intention with Flavors of Lahore is to introduce you to the vibrant tastes of our city. It is an expression of our culture and should be enjoyed with the same enthusiasm with which the people of Lahore enjoy their meals. We want to share the joy of traditional cooking with the world and help keep our culinary heritage alive.

This book takes you on a culinary journey through the city of Lahore. You will be able to discover new dishes that bring exciting flavor profiles to your palate. You will also gain a deeper understanding of the culture of Lahore and its culinary influence. So, let's begin this exciting journey!

We hope you enjoy Flavors of Lahore and that our recipes become a part of your weekly meal plan. We invite you to sample the flavors of Lahore and explore the unique culture of this city. So, get ready to create magical dishes that will bring your family and friends together with the taste of delicious and authentic Lahore cuisine. Bon Appetit!

1. Lahori Charga

Lahori Charga is a traditional Pakistani dish that combines juicy chunks of succulent chicken with a spicy blend of warm spices, aromatics, and tangy tomatoes. Originating from the Punjab region, this tasty dish is sure to tantalize your taste buds with its bold and savory flavor!
Serving: 4
Preparation time: 5
Ready time: 25

Ingredients:
- 1 lb chicken (cut into cubes)
- 2 large tomatoes (chopped)
- 2 large onions (sliced)
- 6 cloves garlic (minced)
- 1 teaspoon chili powder
- 1 tablespoon ground coriander
- 1 teaspoon ground cumin
- 1 teaspoon garam masala
- 2 tablespoons tomato ketchup
- Salt to taste
- 2 tablespoons vegetable oil

Instructions:
1. Heat oil in a large skillet or wok over medium-high heat.
2. Add onions and garlic and sauté for 5 minutes until onions are lightly browned.
3. Add chicken cubes and fry for 5 minutes.
4. Add tomatoes, chili powder, coriander, cumin, garam masala, and tomato ketchup. Fry for 10 minutes.
5. Add salt to taste. Fry for 5 more minutes until all Ingredients are cooked through.
6. Serve hot with rice or naan bread.

Nutrition information:
Calories: 250 kcal
Protein: 23 g
Fat: 11 g

Carbohydrates: 15 g
Sodium: 1.7 mg

2. Nihari

Nihari - An Authentic Example of Pakistani Cuisine
Serving: 4-5 people
Preparation Time: 30 minutes
Ready Time: 2-3 hours

Ingredients:
- 1.5kg of beef shanks (washed and cubed)
- 1/4 cup ghee
- 2 teaspoons ginger-garlic paste
- 2 tablespoons coriander powder
- 2 teaspoons cumin powder
- 2 tablespoons red chili powder
- 1 teaspoon garam masala powder
- 1/4 cup yogurt
- 2 tablespoons of flour
- 2 tomatoes (chopped)
- 4 green chilies (slit lengthwise)
- 2 tablespoons lemon juice
- 2 teaspoons of salt
- 4-5 tablespoons of oil
- 2-3 green cardamoms
- 4-5 cloves
- Water as required

Instructions:
1. Heat the ghee in a large pot over medium-high heat.
2. Add the ginger-garlic paste, coriander powder, cumin powder, red chili powder, and garam masala powder. Saute until aromatic.
3. Add the cubed beef shanks to the pot and mix well to combine.
4. Add the yogurt and flour. Mix everything together and cook for 5 minutes.
5. Add the chopped tomatoes, green chilies, lemon juice, and salt. Give everything a good mix.

6. Add the oil, green cardamoms, and cloves. Stir to combine.

7. Add enough water to cover the Ingredients and bring the pot to a boil. Once boiling, reduce the heat and simmer for 1.5-2 hours, stirring occasionally.

8. Once the beef is tender and the liquid has thickened, turn off the heat and serve hot.

Nutrition information:
Calories: 300kcal
Fat: 16g
Carbs: 9g
Protein: 29g

3. Haleem

Haleem is a tasty dish made out of a mixture of wheat, barley, and meat. It is cooked for several hours, making it an extremely rich and flavorful dish. It is often enjoyed in Ramadan or Eid festivities.

Serving: 8
Preparation Time: 45 minutes
Ready Time: 6 hours

Ingredients:
• 2 ½ cups of wheat, soaked in water overnight
• 1 lb ground beef
• 2 cloves garlic, minced
• 1 medium onion, chopped
• 2 green chillies, chopped
• 4 cups water
• 2 tablespoons oil
• 1 teaspoon salt
• ½ teaspoon turmeric
• ½ teaspoon freshly ground black pepper
• 2 tablespoons garam masala
• 2 tablespoons freshly chopped coriander leaves

Instructions:

1. Heat oil in a large pot over medium-high heat. Add the onions and garlic and cook until soft and fragrant, about 5 minutes.
2. Add the ground beef and cook until browned, about 8 minutes.
3. Add the green chillies, wheat, water, salt, turmeric, and pepper. Stir to combine.
4. Reduce the heat to low and cover the pot. Simmer for 3-4 hours, stirring occasionally.
5. Add the garam masala and coriander leaves and stir to combine. Cook for an additional 1-2 hours, until the mixture is thick and creamy.
6. Serve hot in individual bowls. Enjoy!

Nutrition information: Per Serving: Calories: 478; Total Fat: 11 g; Saturated Fat: 2 g; Protein: 22 g; Carbohydrates: 70 g; Fiber: 6 g; Sodium: 777 mg; Cholesterol: 54 mg

4. Paya Curry

Paya Curry is a deliciously flavorful and slow-cooked Indian dish made from a variety of aromatic spices and herbs with lamb trotters. This South Asian dish is usually served with warm rotis or fluffy white rice.
Serving: 6
Preparation Time: 10 minutes
Ready Time: 2.5 hours

Ingredients:
-2 lbs of lamb trotters
-2 tablespoons of olive oil
-1 large onion, diced
-3 cloves of garlic, minced
-1 tablespoon of ginger paste
-1 teaspoon of cumin powder
-1 teaspoon of coriander powder
-1 teaspoon of red chili powder
-1/2 teaspoon of garam masala
-2 tablespoons of tomato paste
-1/2 cup of coconut milk
-Salt to taste

Instructions:
1. In a large bowl, place lamb trotters. Season with 1 teaspoon of powdered cumin, 1 teaspoon of coriander and 1 teaspoon of red chili powder. Mix to combine.
2. Heat a large saucepan over medium-high heat and add 2 tablespoons of olive oil. Once the oil is hot, add the diced onion and cook until translucent.
3. Add the minced garlic and ginger paste, cooking for another minute.
4. Add the seasoned lamb trotters to the pan and stir. Cook for 5 minutes, stirring occasionally.
5. Add 1/2 cup of coconut milk, stir to combine. Add 1 tablespoon of tomato paste, 1/2 teaspoon of garam masala, and salt to taste. Simmer on low heat for 2 hours.
6. Serve with warm rotis or fluffy white rice. Enjoy!

Nutrition information:
Calories: 336.3 kcal, Carbohydrates: 6.2g, Protein: 24.3g, Fat: 22.6g, Saturated Fat: 5.7g, Cholesterol: 110.8mg, Sodium: 228.1mg, Potassium: 330.4mg, Fiber: 1.5g, Sugar: 1.3g, Vitamin A: 64.3IU, Vitamin C: 2.6mg, Calcium: 30.9mg, Iron: 2.5mg.

5. Lahori Fish Fry

Lahori Fish Fry is a popular dish from the heart of Pakistan. It is made with deep-fried fish prepared with spices and is often served with chutneys. This dish is sure to tantalize your taste buds with its delicious flavors!
Servings: 4
Preparation Time: 10 minutes
Ready Time: 30 minutes

Ingredients:
2 lbs. fish fillet
¾ cup flour
3 tbsps. cornflour
1 tsp. Turmeric powder
1 tsp. ginger and garlic paste
Salt to taste

½ tsp. red chili powder

2 tbsps. coriander powder

2 green chilies, chopped

2 eggs

2 cups of cooking oil

Instructions:
1. In a bowl, mix together the flour, cornflour, turmeric powder, ginger and garlic paste, red chili powder, salt and coriander powder to make a batter.
2. Cut the fish into thick pieces and coat them with the batter.
3. Heat the oil in a deep pan and fry the pieces of fish until golden brown.
4. In a separate bowl, beat the eggs and add the chopped green chilies.
5. Now dip the fried fish pieces in the egg batter and fry again until golden brown.
6. Serve the Lahori Fish Fry with chutney and enjoy!

Nutrition information:
Calories- 307 kcal

Protein- 24.1 g

Fat- 21.3 g

Cholesterol- 114 mg

Sodium- 479 mg

Carbohydrates- 9.6 g

6. Tandoori Chicken

Tandoori Chicken is a classic, flavorful dish from Indian cuisine. It is marinated in a flavorful blend of yogurt, lemon juice, and spices, then cooked in a traditional tandoori oven.

Serving: Serves 4

Preparation Time: 10 minutes

Ready Time: 1 hour (including marination time)

Ingredients:
-1 lb. boneless, skinless chicken thighs
-2 cloves garlic, minced

-2 teaspoons fresh ginger, grated
-2 tablespoons plain yogurt
-1/2 teaspoon ground cumin
-1/2 teaspoon ground coriander
-1/2 teaspoon garam masala
-1/2 teaspoon ground turmeric
-1 tablespoon fresh lemon juice
-Salt and pepper, to taste

Instructions:
1. In a medium bowl, combine garlic, ginger, yogurt, cumin, coriander, garam masala, turmeric, lemon juice, and salt and pepper.
2. Cut chicken into cubes and add to the bowl with the marinade. Stir to ensure each piece of chicken is well coated. Cover and chill in the refrigerator for at least 30 minutes, or up to overnight.
3. Preheat a tandoori oven (or grill) to high heat.
4. Remove chicken from the marinade and thread onto skewers.
5. Place skewers in the tandoori oven and cook for 8 to 10 minutes, turning occasionally, until chicken is cooked through.

Nutrition information: Per Serving—Calories: 161, Total Fat: 7.6g, Saturated Fat: 2.5g, Cholesterol: 79mg, Sodium: 193mg, Carbohydrate: 1.2g, Protein: 20.4g

7. Lahori Karahi

Lahori Karahi is a classic Pakistani dish bursting with flavor. This rich and spicy curry is usually served with naan or chapati.
Serving: 4
Preparation Time: 20 minutes
Ready Time: 45 minutes

Ingredients:
- 1 kg bone-in chicken pieces
- 2 tablespoons vegetable oil
- 2 tablespoons ghee
- 2 onions, sliced
- 2 cloves of garlic, minced

- 1 tablespoon freshly grated ginger
- 1 teaspoon ground cumin
- 1 teaspoon ground coriander
- 1/2 teaspoon ground turmeric
- 1/2 teaspoon chili powder
- 1 teaspoon garam masala
- 1/2 cup tomato puree
- 2 cups water
- Salt and pepper to taste

Instructions:
1. Heat the oil and ghee in a large pot or karahi over medium heat.
2. Add the onions, garlic, and ginger, stirring frequently for 8-10 minutes until the onions are golden brown.
3. Add the spices and stir for 1 minute.
4. Add the chicken pieces and stir for a few minutes until the chicken is lightly browned.
5. Add the tomato puree, stirring until combined.
6. Pour in the water and season with salt and pepper.
7. Cover the pot and simmer for 30 minutes, stirring occasionally.
8. Remove the lid and cook for an additional 15 minutes, stirring occasionally, until the sauce has thickened.
9. Serve hot with naan or chapati.

Nutrition information: Calories per serving: 408, Fat: 24g, Protein: 19g, Carbs: 22g, Fiber: 4g, Sugar: 8g

8. Lahori Tawa Tikka

Lahori Tawa Tikka is a kind of traditional-Pakistani inergetic food - full of flavor made from chicken.
Serving: 4
Preparation Time: 20 minutes
Ready Time: 40 minutes

Ingredients:
- 1 kg chicken breast (cubed)
- 2 tablespoons garlic paste

- 2 tablespoons ginger paste
- 2 tablespoons chili flakes
- 2 tablespoons chaat masala
- 2 tablespoons cumin powder
- 2 tablespoons coriander powder
- 2 tablespoons garam masala
- 2 tablespoons oil
- Salt to taste

Instructions:
1. In a bowl add chicken cubes, garlic paste, ginger paste, chili flakes, chaat masala, cumin powder, coriander powder, and garam masala.
2. Mix all the Ingredients together and marinate for 10 minutes.
3. Now heat oil in a wok or tawa and add the marinated chicken cubes.
4. Saute the chicken cubes until they are cooked all the way through and slightly crispy.
5. Serve the Lahori Tawa Tikka hot with desired condiments of your choice.

Nutrition information: Per serving: Calories 412, Total fat 12.2g (Saturated fat 2.3g), Sodium 376mg, Total carbohydrates 14.6g, Protein 53.2g

9. Lahori Beef Biryani

Lahori Beef Biryani is a flavorful and subtly spiced one-pot dish, originating from the glorious city of Lahore in Pakistan. It is a perfect combination of rice, beef and hearty spices and guaranteed to tantalize your tastebuds.
Serving: 10 servings
Preparation time: 15 minutes
Ready time: 45 minutes

Ingredients:
- 2 tablespoons vegetable oil
- 2 large onions, finely chopped
- 2 tablespoons garlic paste
- 2 tablespoons ginger paste

- 2 teaspoons ground cumin
- 2 teaspoons ground coriander
- 1 teaspoon turmeric
- 1 teaspoon garam masala
- 1 teaspoon red chilli powder
- 500g beef, cut into small cubes
- 1/2 cup yogurt
- 2 cups Basmati rice
- 4 cups water
- 2 large tomatoes, chopped
- 2 tablespoons chopped fresh coriander
- 2 tablespoons chopped fresh mint
- Salt for seasoning

Instructions:
1. Heat the oil in a large skillet over medium heat. Add the onions and fry until golden and softened.
2. Add the garlic and ginger pastes and stir to combine. Then, add the cumin, coriander, turmeric, garam masala, and red chilli powder, and mix to combine.
3. Add the beef cubes and fry until lightly browned. Add the yogurt and combine.
4. Add the Basmati rice and stir to combine. Pour in the water, add the tomatoes, fresh coriander, and fresh mint, and season with salt to taste.
5. Cover the skillet and bring to a boil. Reduce the heat to low and simmer for 30 minutes, or until all of the liquid is absorbed and the rice is cooked.
6. Serve hot with plain yogurt and a salad.

Nutrition information: Calories: 439, Fat: 14.1g, Protein: 28.4g, Carbohydrates: 45.7g, Fiber: 2.2g, Sugar: 3.6g, Cholesterol: 45mg, Sodium: 110mg.

10. Lahori Fried Laham

Lahori Fried Laham is a savoury and delicious dish that originates from Lahore, Pakistan. It is a unique blend of spices and minced meat that is fried in ghee or oil.

Serving: 8
Preparation Time: 15 minutes
Ready Time: 30 minutes

Ingredients:
- 1 lb ground beef
- 2 onions, finely chopped
- 3 cloves of garlic, finely chopped
- 1 teaspoon cumin powder
- 1 teaspoon coriander powder
- 1 teaspoon garam masala powder
- 2 tablespoons red chili powder
- 2 tablespoons plain yogurt
- 2 tablespoons oil or ghee
- Salt to taste

Instructions:
1. In a large bowl, combine the beef with the finely chopped onions and garlic, cumin powder, coriander powder, garam masala powder, red chili powder, plain yogurt and salt to taste.
2. Mix the beef mixture well, cover with cling film and allow to marinate in the refrigerator for 15 minutes.
3. In a large skillet, heat the oil or ghee over medium-high heat.
4. Form small patties from the beef mixture (about 1-2 inch in diameter).
5. Place the patties in the skillet and fry for about 10 minutes, flipping over once during that time.
6. Remove the patties from the skillet and drain onto paper towels.
7. Serve hot with naan or chapati.

Nutrition information:
Calories: 186 kcal, Carbohydrates: 6g, Protein: 11g, Fat: 12g, Saturated Fat: 4g, Cholesterol: 38mg, Sodium: 155mg, Potassium: 285mg, Fiber: 1g, Sugar: 2g, Vitamin A: 343IU, Vitamin C: 4mg, Calcium: 36mg, Iron: 2mg.

11. Lahori Puri Halwa

Lahori Puri halwa is a traditional Punjabi sweet dish that can be served on any special occasion. It is usually served along with puri, a flatbread that is deep fried in oil. This traditional dessert is made up of atta, semolina, and different kinds of dry fruit.

Serving: 5
Preparation Time: 60 minutes
Ready Time: 75 minutes

Ingredients:
- 1/2 cup fine atta
- 1/4 cup semolina
- 1 cup sugar
- 2 tbsp ghee
- 2 tbsp milk
- 2 tsp crushed cardamom
- 2 tsp dry fruit powder
- Ghee and dry fruit for garnish

Instructions:
1. In a large bowl, add the atta and semolina and mix them together.
2. In a separate bowl, add the sugar and ghee and mix them together until the sugar is fully dissolved.
3. Now add the sugar and ghee mixture into the atta and semolina mixture.
4. Next, add the milk and mix them together until it is mixed to form a dough.
5. Now add the crushed cardamom and dry fruit powder to the dough and mix everything together.
6. Take small amounts of the dough and form into small balls.
7. Heat ghee in a frying pan and shallow fry the balls until they are golden brown.
8. Before serving, garnish the halwa with the remaining ghee and dry fruits.

Nutrition information:
Calories: 200
Total Fat: 8 g
Saturated Fat: 4 g
Cholesterol: 20 mg
Sodium: 20 mg

Total Carbohydrates: 27 g
Dietary Fiber: 1 g
Sugars: 12 g
Protein: 3 g

12. Lahori Shahi Tukray

This Lahori Shahi Tukray is an authentic Pakistani snack which is easy to prepare and very delicious.
Serving: 4
Preparation Time: 15 minutes
Ready Time: 45 minutes

Ingredients:
- 2 cups all-purpose flour
- 2 tablespoons ghee or butter
- 1 teaspoon salt
- 1 teaspoon baking powder
- 2 tablespoons sugar
- 3 tablespoons yogurt
- 1/4 cup warm milk
- Cooking oil for frying

Instructions:
1. In a large bowl, combine all-purpose flour, ghee, salt, baking powder, and sugar. Mix until well combined.
2. In a separate bowl, mix together the yogurt and warm milk. Then add to the dry Ingredients and knead into a soft dough.
3. Divide the dough into 15-20 equal portions. Roll out each portion and make a small ball.
4. Heat a large skillet over medium heat and add enough cooking oil to cover the bottom of the pan.
5. Gently place the rolled dough balls in the hot oil and fry until golden brown and crispy.
6. Remove from heat and drain on a paper towel.
7. Serve Lahori Shahi Tukray with your favorite chutney.

Nutrition information:

Serving Size: 1/4 of recipe
Calories: 230
Total Fat: 8 g
Saturated Fat: 3 g
Cholesterol: 10 mg
Sodium: 471 mg
Total Carbohydrate: 36 g
Dietary Fiber: 2 g
Sugar: 5 g
Protein: 6 g

13. Lahori Chana Chaat

Lahori chana chaat is a spicy and savory snack popular in Pakistan. Served hot or cold, this tasty dish is made with boiled chickpeas and various spices.
Serving: 4
Preparation time: 10 minutes
Ready time: 15 minutes

Ingredients:
- 1 cup boiled chickpeas
- 1/2 cup carrots, diced
- 1/2 cup potatoes, diced
- 1/4 cup tomatoes, chopped
- 1 tablespoon red chili powder
- 1/2 teaspoon chaat masala
- 1/2 teaspoon ground cumin
- 2 tablespoons onion, diced
- 2 tablespoons fresh cilantro, chopped
- Juice of one lemon
- Salt to taste

Instructions:
1. In a large bowl, combine cooked chickpeas, carrots, potatoes, tomatoes, red chili powder, chaat masala, ground cumin, onion, cilantro, and lemon juice.
2. Mix well and season with salt to taste.

3. Serve warm or cold.

Nutrition information:
Calories: 160
Fat: 1g
Saturated Fat: 0g
Carbohydrates: 28g
Fiber: 6g
Protein: 7g

14. Lahori Aloo Tikki

Lahori Aloo Tikki is a delicious snack originating from Lahore, Pakistan. It is easy to make and has a unique flavor.
Serving: 4-6
Preparation Time: 15 minutes
Ready Time: 20 minutes

Ingredients:
-3 large Potatoes
-2 Garlic cloves
-3 Green chillies
-1/2 teaspoon of Garam Masala
-Salt to taste
-Oil for deep frying

Instructions:
1. Boil and mash the potatoes.
2. Mince the garlic and the green chillies finely.
3. Add the mashed potatoes, garlic, green chillies, garam masala, and salt to a bowl. Mix the Ingredients properly.
4. Take about ½ cup of the potato mixture and shape into patties.
5. Heat oil in a deep frying pan.
6. Add the tikkis and deep fry until golden brown.
7. Serve warm.

Nutrition information:
Calories: 75

Fat: 5g
Protein: 5g
Carbs: 5g

15. Lahori Piyaz Pakora

Lahori Piyaz Pakora is an exquisite snack from the city of Lahore, Pakistan. It is a savory preparation of fritter-style onion pakoras combined with potatoes and spices.
Serving: 4-5
Preparation time: 15 minutes
Ready time: 30 minutes

Ingredients:
-1 large onion, sliced
-1/2 cup chickpea flour
-2 potatoes, peeled and cubed
-1/2 teaspoon garam masala
-1/4 teaspoon ground red chili powder
-Salt to taste
-Oil for frying

Instructions:
1. In a bowl, combine the chickpea flour, garam masala, ground red chili powder, and salt.
2. Add enough water to make a thick batter.
3. Heat oil in a deep-frying pan on medium heat.
4. Dip the sliced onions and cubed potatoes in the batter, and carefully drop into hot oil.
5. Fry the pakoras until golden brown and crisp.
6. Drain on absorbent paper and serve hot.

Nutrition information:
-カロリー139 kcal
-タンパク質6.6 g
-脂肪2.9 g
-炭水化物25.3 g
-食塩0.78 g

16. Lahori Keema Naan

Lahori Keema Naan has been a famous North Indian dish. This flavorful and juicy dish with minced and spiced meat will tantalize your taste buds. It is served hot and fresh with naan, so you can enjoy with your family.
Serving: 3-4
Preparation Time: 25 minutes
Ready Time: 50 minutes

Ingredients:
- 2 cups Naan bread
- 2 lbs minced beef or lamb
- 2 onions
- 2 cloves of garlic, finely minced
- 2 tablespoons of ginger paste
- 2 teaspoons of garam masala powder
- 1 teaspoon of cumin powder
- ½ teaspoon of red chilli powder
- 2 tablespoons of ghee or butter
- 2 tablespoons of fresh coriander leaves, chopped
- Salt, to taste
- Juice of half a lemon

Instructions:
1. Start by heating a pan and adding ghee.
2. Then, add the minced meat and onions and start frying until the meat has cooked well.
3. Add garlic, ginger paste, garam masala powder, cumin powder, red chilli powder and some salt.
4. Cook for 8-10 minutes, stirring constantly, until the mixture becomes thick and fragrant.
5. Remove from heat and add fresh coriander.
6. Heat a tawa and cook the naan bread for a few minutes until it is golden.
7. Top it off with the cooked meat and lemon juice.
8. Serve warm with a side of chutney or raita.

Nutrition information:
Calories: 225 kcal
Fat: 10 g
Carbohydrates: 16 g
Protein: 16 g
Fiber: 1 g

17. Lahori Kunafa

Lahori Kunafa is a classic and popular Middle Eastern sweet treat made from a rich, buttery pastry filled with a creamy cheese filling and topped with a sprinkle of nuts. This delicious treat is perfect for any special occasion or as a sweet finish to a meal. Serve it warm or cold for a bite of heaven.
Serving: 8
Preparation Time: 10 minutes
Ready Time: 25 minutes

Ingredients:
- 2 cups all-purpose flour
- 2 eggs
- 1 teaspoon baking powder
- ½ cup butter
- 2 cups mozzarella cheese
- 1 cup ricotta cheese
- 2 cups heavy cream
- 2 tablespoons sugar
- ½ cup blanched almonds
- ½ cup melted butter
- Pinch of crushed red pepper

Instructions:
1. Preheat the oven to 375°F.
2. In a medium bowl, combine the flour, baking powder, and eggs.
3. Melt the butter in a small saucepan over low heat. Once melted, add it to the flour mixture and mix to form a dough.
4. Separate the dough into two parts. Roll out each part to form two circles.

5. In a separate bowl, combine the mozzarella, ricotta, cream, sugar, and red pepper. Mix well and spread on top of the two rolled out circles.
6. Bake for 15-20 minutes, until golden brown.
7. Once cooked, remove from the oven and let cool. Spread the melted butter on top and sprinkle with the blanched almonds.

Nutrition information:
Per serving: 640 calories, 36.4g fat, 38.3g protein, 45.6g carbohydrates, 8.5g fiber, 13.5g sugar.

18. Lahori Falooda

Lahori Falooda is a traditional Pakistani dessert made from a mixture of sweet and thickened milk, vermicelli noodles, ice cream, and basil seeds. It is enjoyed all over Pakistan during the hot summer months.
Serving: 4
Preparation Time: 10 minutes
Ready Time: 40 minutes

Ingredients:
• 2 liters Full-cream Milk
• 150grams Vermicelli
• 100grams Sugar
• 2 tablespon Rose syrup
• 6-7 table spoon Basil seeds
• 6 scoops of Vanilla ice cream

Instructions:
1. Boil 2 litres of full-cream milk in a thick-bottomed pan on medium heat.
2. When the milk starts to boil, add 150 grams vermicelli, stirring continuously to avoid lumps.
3. Simmer the mixture for about 30 minutes, or until the vermicelli is cooked and soft.
4. Add in 100 grams of sugar and 2 tablespoons of rose syrup (optional). Stir to dissolve the sugar.
5. Turn off the heat and let the mixture cool slightly.
6. Divide the mixture into 4 equal portions in 4 glasses.

7. Soak 6 tablespoons of basil seeds in a small bowl of warm water for a few minutes. Drain the water and sprinkle the soaked seeds on top of each portion.
8. Top each glass with 1-2 scoops of Vanilla ice cream.
9. Garnish with a few strands of chopped nuts, such as almonds, cashews or pistachios.

Nutrition information: Provides approx. 420 calories per serving. Contains healthy fats, carbohydrates, and proteins.

19. Lahori Rabri

Lahori Rabri is a traditional Pakistani dessert recipe that is made with reduced milk and delicately flavored with nuts and cardamom to give a unique flavor.
Serving: 4
Preparation Time: 10 mins
Ready Time: 4 hours

Ingredients:
-4 cups of whole milk
-2 tablespoons of all-purpose flour
-1/2 cup of thickened cream
-1/4 cup sugar
-1 teaspoon cardamom powder
-2 tablespoons of blanched slivered almonds
-2 tablespoons of blanched pistachios

Instructions:
1. Heat the milk in a large heavy-bottomed saucepan on medium-high heat.
2. When the milk comes to a boil, reduce the heat to a simmer and slowly add the all-purpose flour, stirring continuously.
3. Simmer until the milk is reduced to 1/3 of its original amount, stirring regularly.
4. Add the thickened cream, sugar, cardamom powder, and slivered almonds, stirring to combine.

5. Cook for an additional 5 minutes, stirring continuously, until the mixture is thick and creamy.
6. Transfer the rabri to individual serving bowls, garnish with pistachios, and serve chilled.

Nutrition information: Per serving: 365 calories; 23 g fat (10 g saturated fat; 15 g monounsaturated fat); 72 mg cholesterol; 91 mg sodium; 28 g carbohydrate; 0 g fiber; 8 g sugar; 8 g protein.

20. Lahori Samosa

Lahori Samosa are a delicious Indian snack that is crispy on the outside and flavorful and juicy on the inside. Serve these Samosas as a side with your favorite Indian dishes or as an appetizer.
Serving: 8-10 pieces
Preparation time: 40 minutes
Ready time: 1 hour

Ingredients:
- 2 cups of all purpose flour
- 2 tablespoons of oil
- 1 teaspoon of salt
- Water for kneading
- 4 potatoes boiled, mashed and seasoned
- 2 tablespoons of chopped mint leaves
- ½ teaspoon of garam masala
- ½ teaspoon of asafoetida
- ¼ teaspoon of red chilli powder
- ½ teaspoon of cumin powder
- 2 tablespoons of oil
- Salt to taste

Instructions:
1. In a bowl, mix the flour, oil and salt. Slowly add water and knead to a smooth dough. Cover and keep aside for 20 minutes.
2. Meanwhile, prepare the masala filling. Heat oil in a pan and add the mint leaves. Sauté for few seconds.

3. Next, add the potatoes and all the spices. Mix well and cook for 5 minutes. Allow the filling to cool.
4. Make 8-10 equal portion of the dough. Take a portion and roll into a circle. Cut it into two parts.
5. Take a cone shape out of one part and fill it with the prepared masala filling. Seal the edges with a little water.
6. Heat oil in a pan and deep fry the samosa till it turns golden brown.
7. Drain on an absorbent paper and serve hot with ketchup or chutney.

Nutrition information:
Total Calories: 200 kcal
Carbohydrates: 28g
Protein: 4g
Fat: 11g
Saturated fat: 3g
Fiber: 3g

21. Lahori Chicken Korma

Lahori Chicken Korma is a classic and authentically delicious Pakistani gravy dish. It's the perfect destination for looking for a delightful melody of rich flavours!
Serving: 4
Preparation Time: 15 minutes
Ready Time: 45 minutes

Ingredients:
• 1 kg of boneless chicken cubes
• 1 teaspoon of garlic paste
• 2 tablespoons of ginger paste
• 4 tablespoons of olive oil
• 5 green chillies (halved)
• 2 teaspoons of cumin powder
• 2 teaspoons of chilli powder
• 1 teaspoon of coriander powder
• 2 tablespoons of freshly-chopped coriander leaves
• 2 tablespoons of fresh cream
• 1 cup of yoghurt

- 2 onions sliced thinly
- 2 tomatoes cut into wedges
- 1 teaspoon of garam masala
- Salt to taste

Instructions:
1. Heat the oil in a heavy-bottomed pan or a pressure cooker.
2. Add the onions and sauté until golden brown.
3. Add the ginger and garlic pastes and sauté for a few more minutes.
4. Add the chicken cubes, green chillies, cumin, chilli, and coriander powders, and salt to taste.
5. Cover the pan or the pressure cooker with a lid and let the chicken cook on medium heat for 10 minutes.
6. Add the yoghurt, tomatoes, fresh cream, and 1/2 cup of hot water and mix all the Ingredients together well.
7. Let the mixture simmer for 25 minutes until the chicken is cooked through properly.
8. Add the garam masala and coriander leaves and mix well.
9. Heat for 5 minutes and turn off the flame.

Nutrition information (approx.):
- Calories: 295 Kcal
- Fat: 18.9 g
- Saturated Fat: 6.2 g
- Carbohydrates: 8.9 g
- Sugar: 5.2 g
- Fiber: 2.4 g
- Protein: 24.4 g
- Cholesterol: 68 mg
- Sodium: 270 mg

22. Lahori Bhindi Masala

Lahori Bhindi Masala is a traditional Pakistani dish, made with okra and a flavorful blend of spices. It's a vegan dish usually eaten with fresh chapatis or parathas.
Serving: 6 people
Preparation Time: 10 minutes

Ready Time: 25 minutes

Ingredients:
- 2 tablespoons cooking oil
- 1kg fresh okra, washed, trimmed and cut into thin slices
- 2 onions, finely chopped
- 1 tablespoon grated fresh ginger
- 1 tablespoon cumin
- 1 teaspoon turmeric
- 2 tablespoons ground coriander
- 1 teaspoon chilli powder
- 1/2 teaspoon black pepper
- 2 tomatoes, roughly chopped
- 2 tablespoons freshly chopped coriander
- Salt to taste

Instructions:
1. Heat the oil in a frying pan over medium heat. Add the okra and fry for 8-10 minutes or until golden brown.
2. Add the onion to the pan and fry for 3-4 minutes or until softened.
3. Add the ginger, cumin, turmeric, coriander, chilli powder and black pepper. Fry for 1 minute.
4. Add the tomatoes and fry for another 2 minutes.
5. Add the freshly chopped coriander and salt to taste and mix well. Cook for another 2 minutes.
6. Serve with fresh chapatis or parathas.

Nutrition information: per serving, Lahori Bhindi Masala has approximate therm value of 162 cal, 7.4 g fat, 21.1 g carbohydrates, and 3.3 g protein.

23. Lahori Aloo Gosht

Lahori Aloo Gosht is a traditional and savory Pakistani dish usually prepared with beef or lamb and potatoes. The flavorful and aromatic meat and potato stew is served with steamed rice, roti, and naan.
Serving: 4-6
Preparation Time: 15 minutes

Ready Time: 45 minutes

Ingredients:
- 2 tablespoons vegetable oil
- 2 pounds beef, cubed
- 1 onion, chopped
- 4 cloves garlic, minced
- 1 teaspoon ground coriander
- 2 teaspoons ground cumin
- 2 tablespoons red chili powder
- 3 tablespoons tomato paste
- 1 teaspoon ground turmeric
- 2 potatoes, cubed
- 2 cups beef stock
- Salt and black pepper, to taste
- Freshly chopped cilantro, for garnish

Instructions:
1. Heat oil in a large pot or dutch oven over medium-high heat.
2. Add beef and onion and cook until beef is browned, about 8 minutes.
3. Add garlic, coriander, cumin, red chili powder, tomato paste, and turmeric to the pot and cook until fragrant, about 1 minute.
4. Add potatoes and beef stock to the pot and bring to a boil.
5. Reduce heat to a simmer, cover the pot, and cook until beef is tender, about 30 minutes.
6. Remove the lid and season with salt and black pepper.
7. Garnish with freshly chopped cilantro and serve.

Nutrition information: Calories: 418, Total Fat: 18g, Saturated fat: 7g, Polyunsaturated fat: 2g, Monounsaturated fat: 6g, Cholesterol: 117mg, Sodium: 249mg, Potassium: 516mg, Carbohydrates: 26g, Dietary fiber: 2g, Sugar: 3g, Protein: 34g.

24. Lahori Chicken Tikka Masala

Lahori Chicken Tikka Masala is a classic, delicious and spicy curry dish popular throughout Pakistan. This flavorful curry dish is cooked in a traditional and authentic method with spice-laden Ingredients.

Serving: 4-6
Preparation time: 30 minutes
Ready time: 55 minutes

Ingredients:
- 4 chicken thighs, skinless
- ¼ cup plain Greek yogurt
- 2 cloves garlic, minced
- 2 teaspoons ginger paste
- 2 tablespoons ground cumin
- 2 tablespoons ground coriander
- 2 tablespoons garam masala
- 2 teaspoons chili powder
- 1 teaspoon ground turmeric
- 1 tablespoon paprika
- Salt, to taste
- 2 tablespoons ghee or vegetable oil
- 1 large onion, finely chopped
- 2 bay leaves
- 1 teaspoon freshly grated ginger
- 2 teaspoons tomato purée
- 2 large tomatoes, pureed
- 1 teaspoon sugar
- 1 can tomato sauce
- 2 tablespoons heavy cream
- 2 tablespoons chopped fresh cilantro

Instructions:
1. In a large bowl, combine the chicken, yogurt, garlic, ginger paste, cumin, coriander, garam masala, chili powder, turmeric, paprika, and salt. Mix until the Ingredients form a thick paste.
2. Heat the ghee or oil in a large skillet or Dutch oven over medium-high heat. Add the chicken mixture and stir, frying the chicken on all sides until golden and cooked through (about 10 minutes).
3. Remove the chicken from the pan and set aside. Add the onion, bay leaves, and freshly grated ginger to the skillet. Sauté until the onion is softened and golden (about 5 minutes).
4. Return the chicken to the pan. Add the tomato purée, tomato sauce, and sugar. Stir to combine. Bring the mixture to a simmer and cook over

low heat, stirring occasionally, until the sauce has thickened (about 15 minutes).
5. Stir in the heavy cream and cilantro. Simmer for a few minutes, until heated through.

Nutrition information: Serving Size: 1/6
Calories: 230; Total Fat: 12.2g; Cholesterol: 58mg; Sodium: 192mg; Total Carbs: 12.6g; Protein: 15.2g.

25. Lahori Paye

Lahori Paye is a traditional Pakistani dish made from slow-cooked goat trotters with aromatic spices. It is often eaten with fresh-baked naan bread.
Serving: 4
Preparation Time: 25 min
Ready Time: 3 hours

Ingredients:
2 lbs goat trotters
2 onions
5 cloves of garlic
1 inch of ginger root
2 tablespoons of vegetable oil
1 teaspoon of cumin powder
2 teaspoons of coriander powder
2 teaspoons of garam masala powder
Water as required
Salt to taste

Instructions:
1. Wash goat trotters and place them in a large pot.
2. Finely chop onions, garlic, and ginger and add them to the pot.
3. Add the vegetable oil and let it heat up for a few minutes.
4. Add cumin powder, coriander powder and garam masala powder to the pot and stir well.
5. Add enough water to just cover the trotters.
6. Cover the pot and leave it to cook on a low heat for 3 hours.

7. Check the trotters for tenderness by pressing it with a spoon, if tender, add salt to taste.
8. Serve the dish with fresh-baked naan bread.

Nutrition information: Per serving (around 125 g): 190 calories, 17 g fat, 4 g saturated fat, 0 g trans fat, 5 g protein, 5 g carbohydrate, 1 g fiber.

26. Lahori Chicken Biryani

Lahori Chicken Biryani is a very popular Pakistani dish, prized for its flavorful aroma and its fragrant and zesty flavor profile. This popular recipe combines spicy chicken and savory basmati rice and is sure to please.
Serving: 4-6
Preparation Time: 25 minutes
Ready Time: 1 hour 35 minutes

Ingredients:
- 2 cups long grain basmati rice
- 6 boneless, skinless chicken thighs
- 2 tablespoons vegetable oil
- 2 teaspoons garam masala
- 1 teaspoon ground cumin
- 1 teaspoon ground coriander
- 1 teaspoon ground turmeric
- 1 tablespoon kosher salt
- 2 tablespoons freshly grated ginger
- 2 cloves garlic, minced
- 4 green chilies, finely chopped
- 2 medium onions, finely chopped
- 3/4 cup plain yogurt
- 2 tablespoons fresh cilantro, chopped
- 2 tablespoons fresh mint, chopped
- 1 teaspoon ground black pepper
- 1 teaspoon chili powder
- 2 tablespoons chopped almonds
- 2 tablespoons chopped cashews

- 2 tablespoons raisins
- 2 tablespoons vegetable oil

Instructions:
1. Begin by rinsing the basmati rice in several changes of cold water until the water runs clear.
2. In a medium bowl, combine the garam masala, cumin, coriander, turmeric, salt, ginger, garlic, and green chilies. Mix together well.
3. Rub the mixture onto the chicken and let it marinate for 15 minutes.
4. Heat the oil in a large skillet and add the onions. Saute until golden brown.
5. Add the chicken and cook until the chicken is browned.
6. Add the yogurt and cook for an additional 5 minutes.
7. In a large pot, add the soaked rice, cilantro, mint, black pepper, chili powder, almonds, cashews, raisins, and 2 tablespoons of oil. Mix together and cover.
8. In a separate pot, bring 4 cups of water to a boil.
9. Add the chicken mixture to the rice and mix together.
10. Reduce the heat and pour the boiling water over the rice. Cover and simmer for 15 minutes.
11. Remove from heat and let sit for 10 minutes.
12. Serve hot.

Nutrition information: Serving size: 1 cup, Calories: 350, Total fat: 19 g, Total carbohydrates: 26 g, Dietary fiber: 2 g, Protein: 17 g

27. Lahori Kheer

Lahori Kheer is a savory and creamy Pakistani dessert made with milk, basmati rice, sugar, and cardamom.
Serving: 6
Preparation Time: 10 minutes
Ready Time: 40 minutes

Ingredients:
- 6 cups Milk
- 1/2 cup Basmati Rice
- 1/4 cup Sugar

- 2-3 Cardamom pods, crushed
- 1/4 cup Raisins
- 1/2 cup Chopped Nuts (almonds, pistachios, cashew)

Instructions:
1. In a large saucepan, bring the milk to a boil over medium heat and then reduce the heat to low.
2. Meanwhile, rinse the rice and add it to the boiling milk, stirring occasionally.
3. Add the sugar and cardamom and simmer until the rice is tender and the mixture is creamy, stirring occasionally for 25-30 minutes.
4. Remove from the heat and stir in the raisins and nuts.
5. Serve hot or cold.

Nutrition information: (Based on 1 Serving)
- Calories: 225
- Fat: 8g
- Carbohydrates: 30g
- Protein: 7g

28. Lahori Chicken Pulao

Lahori Chicken Pulao is a flavorful, spicy Pakistani rice dish cooked with chicken, tomatoes, and a blend of fragrant spices.
Serving: 4-6
Preparation time: 20 minutes
Ready time: 45 minutes

Ingredients:
- 2 tablespoons vegetable oil
- 4 boneless, skinless chicken breasts, cut into cubes
- 4 peeled and diced tomatoes
- 2 teaspoons ground cumin
- 2 teaspoons ground coriander
- 1 teaspoon ground turmeric
- 1 teaspoon ground red chili pepper
- 1 teaspoon garlic paste
- 1 teaspoon ginger paste

- 2 cups basmati rice
- 4 cups chicken broth
- 1/2 teaspoon salt

Instructions:
1. Heat the vegetable oil in a large pot over medium-high heat.
2. Add the chicken cubes to the pot and cook until golden, about 5 minutes.
3. Add the tomatoes, cumin, coriander, turmeric, chili pepper, garlic and ginger pastes to the pot and cook for 2 minutes.
4. Add the rice and stir to combine.
5. Add the chicken broth and salt and bring to a boil.
6. Reduce the heat to low, cover, and cook until the rice is tender and the liquid has been absorbed, about 25 minutes. Fluff with a fork before serving.

Nutrition information:
Calories: 400 kcal
Carbs: 54 g
Protein: 21 g
Fat: 11 g

29. Lahori Koftay

Lahori Koftay is a traditional Pakistani dish. This beef and potato dish is cooked in a variety of ways and is served in thick tomato-based gravy.
Serving: 4
Preparation Time: 15 minutes
Ready Time: 40 minutes

Ingredients:
- 500g beef mince
- 4 potatoes, par-boiled and mashed
- 2 large onions, diced
- 2 cloves garlic, crushed
- 1 teaspoon ground coriander
- 1 teaspoon ground cumin
- 1 teaspoon garam masala

- 2 green chillies, sliced
- 2 tablespoons vegetable oil
- 2 tablespoons fresh coriander leaves, chopped
- 2 tomatoes, diced
- 1 cup beef stock
- 1 teaspoon beef masala
- Salt and pepper to taste

Instructions:
1. Heat oil in a large pan over medium-high heat.
2. Add the onions and garlic and cook until softened, about 5 minutes.
3. Add the beef mince and cook until it is browned, about 10 minutes.
4. Add the ground coriander, cumin, garam masala, beef masala, green chilies, salt, and pepper and cook for another 5 minutes.
5. Add the potatoes and tomato and stir to combine.
6. Add the beef stock and bring to a simmer.
7. Reduce the heat to low, cover the pan, and simmer for 25 minutes.
8. Add the fresh coriander leaves and serve.

Nutrition information:
Calories: 360kcal, Protein: 24g, Carbohydrates: 22g, Fat: 19g, Sodium: 372mg.

30. Lahori Mutton Handi

Lahori Mutton Handi is a classic punjabi dish originating from Lahore, Pakistan. It is a delicious combination of mutton, spices, and gravy that is sure to tantalize the taste buds of every spice lover.
Serving: Serves 4-5
Preparation Time: 10 minutes
Ready Time: 40 minutes

Ingredients:
- 2 ½ lb mutton
- ¼ cup vegetable oil
- 2 medium onions (sliced)
- 2 tablespoon ginger-garlic paste
- 2 tablespoons red chili powder

- 1 teaspoon garam masala
- Few drops of food color (optional)
- 3 cups warm water
- Salt to taste

Instructions:
1. In a steel or clay pot, heat oil over medium heat.
2. Add sliced onions and sauté until light brown.
3. Add mutton and cook for 20 minutes, stirring intermittently.
4. Add in the ginger garlic paste, red chili powder, garam masala, and food color (optional).
5. Cook for 5 more minutes while stirring.
6. Add warm water and cover pot and simmer until mutton is tender and cooked (about 20 minutes).
7. Once the mutton is tender add salt to taste.
8. Simmer for a few more minutes until gravy thickens.

Nutrition information:
- Calories: 519 kcal
- Protein: 45.4 g
- Total Fat: 34.7 g
- Carbohydrates: 4.2 g
- Fiber: 0.9 g
- Sodium: 551 mg

31. Lahori Chole

Lahori Chole is a spicy, flavourful and savoury delicacy served in all parts of India. It is made with chickpeas and a variety of spices and herbs.
Serving: 4
Preparation time: 10 minutes
Ready time: 20 minutes

Ingredients:
- 1 cup dried chickpeas
- 3 tablespoons vegetable oil
- 1 teaspoon cumin seeds
- 1 teaspoon chopped ginger

- 1 large onion, chopped
- 2-3 chopped green chillies
- 2 green cardamoms
- 1 teaspoon ground coriander
- 1/2 teaspoon chilli powder
- 1/2 teaspoon garam masala
- 2 cloves garlic, minced
- 1 teaspoon tomato paste
- salt to taste
- 2 teaspoons chopped coriander

Instructions:
1. Soak the chickpeas overnight and cook in boiling water for about 15 minutes.
2. Heat the oil in a large saucepan over medium heat and add the cumin seeds.
3. Add the ginger, onion, and green chillies, and cook until the onion is lightly browned.
4. Add the cardamoms, coriander, chilli powder, garam masala, garlic, tomato paste, and salt. Cook for 1 minute.
5. Add the cooked chickpeas and stir to combine.
6. Cook until all the spices are well blended with the chickpeas.
7. Sprinkle the chopped coriander and serve.

Nutrition information:
Calories: 260, Total Fat: 8g, Saturated Fat: 1g, Cholesterol: 0mg, Sodium: 320mg, Carbohydrates: 36g, Fiber: 14g, Sugar: 11g, Protein: 11g

32. Lahori Chicken Shawarma

Lahori Chicken Shawarma is a popular dish that originates from the Pakistan city of Lahore. It is a wrap filled with succulent chicken, veggies, and an array of spices that provide a delicious and flavorful meal.
Serving: Makes 4 servings
Preparation Time: 15 minutes
Ready Time: 45 minutes

Ingredients:

- 2 cups cooked shredded chicken
- 1/4 cup vegetable oil
- 2 tablespoons garlic paste
- 2 tablespoons ginger paste
- 1/2 teaspoon cumin powder
- 1 teaspoon coriander powder
- 1/2 teaspoon red chilli powder
- Salt to taste
- 2 tablespoons lemon juice
- 2 tablespoons white vinegar
- 2 tablespoons chopped cilantro
- 4 chapattis
- 2 cups thinly-sliced onions
- 1/2 cup finely-chopped tomatoes
- 2 tablespoons finely-chopped green chilli peppers
- 1/4 cup sliced cucumber

Instructions:
1. Heat the oil in a large pan over medium heat.
2. Add the garlic and ginger pastes, cumin powder, coriander powder, red chilli powder, and salt. Stir until fragrant.
3. Add the shredded chicken and sauté until lightly browned.
4. Add the lemon juice, white vinegar, and cilantro, and stir to combine.
5. Place the chapattis on a plate and spread the chicken mixture onto the chapattis.
6. Top with the onions, tomatoes, green chilli peppers, and cucumber.
7. Serve and enjoy.

Nutrition information (per serving): Calories: 280; Total Fat: 15 g; Sodium: 540 mg; Carbohydrates: 18 g; Protein: 17 g; Fiber: 2 g.

33. Lahori Mutton Karahi

Lahori Mutton Karahi is a classic traditional Pakistani dish, originating from the city of Lahore. It is an easy-to-prepare, delicious curry of mutton in a rich fragrant gravy with a tang of ginger and tomato.
Serving: 4
Preparation time: 15 mins

Ready time: 1 hour

Ingredients:
- 1 kg Lamb mutton
- 1 large onion
- 1 tomato
- 2- 3 garlic cloves
- 2 teaspoons ginger paste
- 2 green chillies
- 2 tablespoons coriander leaves
- 1 teaspoon turmeric powder
- 2 tablespoons vegetable oil
- Salt to taste

Instructions:
1. Wash the mutton pieces thoroughly and pat them dry using kitchen towels.
2. Finely chop the onion, garlic and tomato.
3. Heat the oil in a large pot, and add the onion. Fry till golden brown.
4. Add the chopped garlic and ginger paste and fry for 2 minutes.
5. Add the mutton pieces and fry for 10 minutes.
6. Add the chopped tomato, chili, turmeric powder and salt to taste. Stir for a few minutes.
7. Lower the heat and cover the pot with a lid. Allow the mutton to cook till tender.
8. Once the mutton is cooked, add the chopped coriander leaves. Simmer for 10 minutes.
9. Serve hot with steamed rice or chapati.

Nutrition information:
Calories: 510, Carbohydrates: 29g, Protein: 37g, Fat: 28g, Cholesterol: 105mg, Sodium: 316mg, Potassium: 1113mg, Fiber: 5g, Sugar: 9.9g, Vitamin A: 440IU, Vitamin C: 28.2mg, Calcium: 90mg, Iron: 5.8mg.

34. Lahori Paneer Tikka

Lahori Paneer Tikka is a delicious and flavourful desi dish that is popular in North India. It is made with marinated paneer cubes and cooked in a grill or tandoor. This mouth-watering delicacy is highly aromatic and has a pleasing smoky flavour.

Serving: 4

Preparation time: 20 minutes

Ready time: 20 minutes

Ingredients:
- 250 grams paneer, cubed
- 1 tablespoon ginger-garlic paste
- 2 tablespoon hung curd
- 2 tablespoon besan
- 2 tablespoon oil
- 2 teaspoon chaat masala
- 1 teaspoon red chilli powder
- 2 teaspoon lemon juice
- 2 tablespoon mint chutney
- Salt, to taste

Instructions:

1. In a bowl, mix together the hung curd, ginger-garlic paste, besan, oil, chaat masala, red chilli powder, lemon juice, mint chutney and salt.

2. Add the cubed paneer to the marinade and mix until the cubes are well coated.

3. Let it marinate for at least 15 minutes.

4. Preheat a grill or tandoor and place the cubes on skewers.

5. Place the skewers in the tandoor or on the grill and cook until the cubes turn golden.

6. Serve hot with chutney.

Nutrition information: Per serving: Energy – 250 kcal, Total Fat – 12 g, Saturated Fat – 4 g, Cholesterol – 5 mg, Sodium – 50 mg, Carbohydrates – 23 g, Dietary Fiber – 1 g, Sugar – 5 g, Protein – 13 g.

35. Lahori Seekh Kebab

Deliciously crispy and golden on the outside, these Lahori Seekh Kebabs are made with fragrant spices, juicy lamb mince, parsley, and mint. Serve these as party appetizers, with creamy mint yogurt dip or lemon wedges for a delicious and memorable feast.

Serving - 10

Preparation Time - 25 minutes

Ready Time - 30 minutes

Ingredients:
- 500g lamb mince
- 2 tablespoons finely chopped fresh parsley
- 2 tablespoons finely chopped fresh mint
- 1 teaspoon cumin powder
- 1 teaspoon garam masala
- 1 teaspoon coriander powder
- 2 tablespoons plain yogurt
- 2 medium onions, finely chopped
- 2 cloves garlic, crushed
- 2 teaspoons freshly grated ginger
- 2 tablespoons oil
- Salt, to taste

Instructions:
1. In a large bowl, combine the lamb mince, parsley, mint, cumin powder, garam masala, coriander powder, yogurt, onions, garlic, ginger and a pinch of salt.
2. Divide the mixture into 10-12 equal parts and shape each part into a flat sausage shape.
3. Heat the oil in a large frying pan over medium-high heat.
4. Add the seekh kebabs and cook for 4-5 minutes each side, or until golden and cooked through.
5. Transfer to a plate and serve hot with mint yogurt dip or lemon wedges. Enjoy!

Nutrition information -
Amount Per Serving: Calories: 213 kcal

Carbohydrates: 5.1g

Protein: 20.7g

Fat: 11.9g

36. Lahori Tandoori Naan

This delicious recipe for Lahori Tandoori Naan is inspired by the traditional street food of Lahore, Pakistan. It's delicious, full of flavor, and easy to make.

Serving: 4
Preparation Time: 20 minutes
Ready Time: 45 minutes

Ingredients:
- 2 cups all-purpose flour
- 1 teaspoon baking powder
- 1 teaspoon salt
- 1 teaspoon sugar
- 3 tablespoons vegetable oil
- 1/2 cup warm water
- 2 tablespoons plain yogurt
- 4 tablespoons melted butter
- 2 tablespoons garlic paste

Instructions:
1. In a large bowl, mix together the flour, baking powder, salt, and sugar, and stir to combine.
2. Make a well in the center and add the vegetable oil, warm water, and plain yogurt. Mix until a soft dough forms.
3. Knead the dough for 8 minutes, then cover and let rest for 30 minutes.
4. Preheat the oven to 350 degrees F (175 degrees C).
5. Divide the dough into 4 equal pieces, and roll each piece into a flat circle about 1/4 inch thick.
6. Arrange on a baking sheet and brush with the melted butter and garlic paste.
7. Bake for 18-20 minutes, or until golden brown.

Nutrition information:
- Calories: 302 kcal
- Carbohydrates: 39 g
- Protein: 5 g
- Fat: 14 g
- Sodium: 460 mg

37. Lahori Chicken Boti

Lahori Chicken Boti is a deliciously marinated and grilled Pakistani dish that is flavorful and tender.
Serving: 6 people
Preparation time: 20 minutes
Ready time: 25 minutes

Ingredients:
• 2 pounds skinless chicken breasts, cut into 1-inch cubes
• 2 tablespoons garlic paste
• 2 tablespoons lemon juice
• 1/2 teaspoon ground cumin
• 1/2 teaspoon cayenne pepper
• 1/2 teaspoon ground cinnamon
• 1/4 cup vegetable oil
• Salt and pepper to taste

Instructions:
1. In a medium bowl, combine garlic paste, lemon juice, cumin, cayenne pepper, cinnamon, vegetable oil, salt, and pepper.
2. Add the chicken cubes to the marinade and mix until the chicken pieces are evenly coated. Refrigerate for 10 to 20 minutes.
3. Preheat an outdoor grill for medium-high heat.
4. Thread the chicken cubes onto skewers and grill for 6 to 8 minutes, turning often, or until the chicken is cooked through and no longer pink.

Nutrition information: Per Serving: 149 calories; 7.7 g fat; 1.0 g carbohydrates; 18.3 g protein; 63 mg cholesterol; 200 mg sodium.

38. Lahori Methi Aloo

Lahori Methi Aloo is a flavorful side dish from the city of Lahore in Punjab, Pakistan. It's a beloved dish enjoyed by adults and kids alike, and is easy and quick to make.
Serving: 4 servings
Preparation time: 10 minutes

Ready time: 25 minutes

Ingredients:
- 4 medium potatoes, cubed
- 1 large onion, chopped
- 2 cloves garlic, minced
- 2 tablespoons fresh fenugreek (methi) leaves
- 1 teaspoon cumin seeds
- 1 teaspoon coriander powder
- 1 teaspoon red chili powder
- 1 teaspoon garam masala
- 2 tablespoons oil
- Salt and black pepper, to taste

Instructions:
1. Heat the oil in a large skillet over medium-high heat.
2. Add the onion and cook until it is softened and lightly browned.
3. Add the garlic and cumin seeds, and cook for 1 minute, stirring.
4. Add the potatoes and cook for 8–10 minutes, stirring occasionally, until they are lightly browned and crisp.
5. Add the fenugreek leaves, coriander powder, red chili powder, garam masala, salt, and black pepper. Stir to combine and cook for 1–2 minutes.
6. Cover and cook for 10 minutes, stirring occasionally, or until the potatoes are cooked through and fork-tender.

Nutrition information:
Calories: 211 kcal; Protein: 3.9 g; Fat: 8.7 g; Carbs: 29.6 g; Fiber: 3.3 g; Sugar: 2.4 g; Sodium: 60 mg

39. Lahori Fish Curry

Lahori Fish Curry is a traditional specialty of the city of Lahore, in Pakistan. It is an aromatic and delicious seafood dish that features a rich, spicy tomato base with large chunks of fresh fish.
Serving: 4-6 people
Preparation time: 25 minutes
Ready time: 45 minutes

Ingredients:
- 3-4 pounds of fish, cut into large pieces
- 2-3 tomatoes, diced
- 1 onion, diced
- 2 tablespoons of minced ginger
- 2 tablespoons of garam masala
- 2 tablespoons of cumin
- 2 tablespoons of coriander
- 2-3 cloves of garlic, minced
- 2 tablespoons of turmeric
- 2 teaspoons of red chili flakes
- 2 tablespoons of vegetable oil
- Salt and pepper to taste

Instructions:
1. Heat the oil in a large saucepan over medium heat.
2. Add the onions and garlic and sauté for 5 minutes until soft.
3. Add the tomatoes and cook for an additional 3 minutes.
4. Add the ginger, spices, and salt and pepper. Cook for 2 minutes, stirring often.
5. Add the fish pieces and stir to combine. Cook for 10 minutes, stirring occasionally.
6. Add 1 cup of water and bring to a boil. Then reduce to a simmer and cook for an additional 20 minutes or until the fish is cooked through.
7. Serve hot with steamed rice or naan.

Nutrition information: Calories: 170; Protein: 21g; Carbohydrates: 8g; Fat: 7g; Fiber: 2g; Cholesterol: 55mg; Sodium: 200mg.

40. Lahori Dum Aloo

Lahori Dum Aloo is a classic Pakistani curry dish made with small baby potatoes cooked in a yoghurt and spice base. Rich and creamy, it is a perfect side dish for any feast.
Serving: 4
Preparation time: 15 minutes
Ready time: 45 minutes

Ingredients:
- 8-10 small baby potatoes
- 2 onions, chopped
- 2-3 garlic cloves, chopped
- 2 green chillies, chopped
- 2 teaspoons ginger-garlic paste
- 1 teaspoon chilli powder
- 1/2 teaspoon turmeric powder
- 1/2 teaspoon coriander powder
- 1/4 cup Greek yoghurt
- Salt, to taste
- 2-3 tablespoons oil
- 1 teaspoon garam masala
- Fresh coriander, for garnish

Instructions:
1. Boil the potatoes in salted water for 10-15 minutes until they are tender. Drain and set aside.
2. Heat the oil in a large saucepan over medium heat. Add the onions, garlic, green chillies and ginger-garlic paste and cook for 5 minutes until the onions are golden brown.
3. Add the chilli powder, turmeric powder and coriander powder and cook for 2 minutes, stirring continuously.
4. Add the boiled potatoes to the pan and stir to coat them in the spices, then add the yoghurt and salt. Lower the heat and cook for 10 minutes until the potatoes are tender and the gravy has thickened.
5. Add the garam masala and stir well. Garnish with fresh coriander leaves and serve hot.

Nutrition information:
per serving -
Calories: 197 kcal
Carbs: 24 g
Protein: 4.6 g
Fat: 10.3 g
Saturated fat: 1.5 g
Fiber: 2.9 g

41. Lahori Mutton Pulao

Lahori Mutton Pulao is a delicious pulao recipe from the Lahore city of Pakistan. It is a classic combo of succulent mutton and fragrant rice all spiced up wonderfully.
Serving: 4-5
Preparation time: 15 mins
Ready time: 40 mins

Ingredients:
- 1 kilogram mutton, cut into medium pieces
- 2 cups basmati rice
- 2 large onions,chopped
- 3 tablespoons ghee
- 5-6 cloves
- 1 teaspoon cumin
- 6-7 cardamoms
- 4-5 diced tomatoes
- 2 tablespoons ginger garlic paste
- 2 teaspoons red chili powder
- 1 teaspoon garam masala powder
- 1 teaspoon cumin powder
- 1 teaspoon turmeric powder
- 2-3 green chilies, finely chopped
- 1/2 cup of chopped fresh coriander
- Salt to taste

Instructions:
1. Heat the ghee in a heavy-bottomed pot over medium flame.
2. Add the cloves, cardamoms, and cumin and let it sputter.
3. Add the chopped onions and sauté for a few minutes until golden brown.
4. Add the ginger garlic paste and green chilies and sauté for a minute.
5. Add the mutton pieces and cook for 8-10 minutes.
6. Add the red chili powder, garam masala powder, cumin powder, turmeric powder and salt and cook for 5 minutes.
7. Now add the diced tomatoes and mix well and cook for 10 minutes.
8. Add 2 cups of water and bring it to a boil.
9. Add the basmati rice and mix well.

10. Cover and cook on low flame for 15 minutes or till the rice is done and all the water is absorbed.

11. Finally, garnish with chopped coriander and serve with raita or salad.

Nutrition information:
Calories: 362, Carbohydrates: 38g, Protein: 15g, Fat: 14g, Saturated Fat: 4.8g, Sodium: 354mg, Potassium: 317mg, Fiber: 2.7g, Sugar: 2.2g, Vitamin A: 539IU , Vitamin C: 5.4mg, Calcium: 56mg, Iron: 1.8mg

42. Lahori Mix Vegetable Curry

Lahori Mix Vegetable Curry is a delicious curry packed with lots of flavour and loaded with many vegetables. It is a very popular dish from Lahore, Pakistan.

Serving: 4-6
Preparation time: 10 minutes
Ready time: 25 minutes

Ingredients:
- 2 tablespoons of oil
- 2 large onions, finely chopped
- 4 cloves garlic, minced
- 2 tablespoons of ginger, minced
- 1 tablespoon of ground cumin
- 1 teaspoon of ground coriander
- 1 teaspoon of ground turmeric
- 1 teaspoon of garam masala
- 1 teaspoon of ground black pepper
- 2 cups of red lentils
- 1 teaspoon of sea salt
- 2 cups of frozen peas
- 1 small cauliflower, cut into small florets
- 2 large potatoes, cut into small cubes
- 1 large carrots, chopped
- 1 (14-ounce) can of diced tomatoes
- 3 cups of vegetable broth
- 1/4 cup of cilantro leaves

Instructions:
1. Heat oil in a large pot over medium-high heat.
2. Add onions, garlic and ginger to the pot and sauté for 2-3 minutes until fragrant.
3. Add the cumin, coriander, turmeric, garam masala and black pepper and cook for 1 minute, stirring constantly.
4. Add the lentils and sea salt and stir to combine.
5. Add the peas, cauliflower, potatoes and carrots and stir to combine.
6. Add the diced tomatoes and vegetable broth and bring to a boil.
7. Reduce the heat to low and let the curry simmer for 15-20 minutes, stirring occasionally.
8. Remove the pot from the heat and stir in the cilantro leaves.

Nutrition information:
Calories: 336, Total Fat: 4g, Saturated Fat: 0.5g, Trans Fat: 0g, Polyunsaturated Fat: 2g, Monounsaturated Fat: 1g, Cholesterol: 0mg, Sodium: 825mg, Total Carbohydrates: 57g, Dietary Fiber: 17g, Sugars: 8g, Protein: 17g.

43. Lahori Mutton Curry

Lahori Mutton Curry is a spicy and delicious dish which is often served by street vendors in Pakistan as a popular snack. It is a great dish to serve during family gatherings or as a special occasion meal.
Serving: 8
Preparation time: 15 minutes
Ready time: 45 minutes

Ingredients:
- 2 lbs. mutton, cut into cubes
- 4 tablespoons ghee (clarified butter)
- 2 large onions, chopped
- 2 tablespoons ginger-garlic paste
- 2 tablespoons coriander powder
- 2 teaspoons cumin powder
- 1 teaspoon turmeric powder
- 3 large tomatoes, chopped
- 1/2 teaspoon garam masala (ground spices)

- 2 tablespoons ground red chili
- Salt, to taste
- 2 tablespoons chopped fresh cilantro, for garnish

Instructions:
1. Heat ghee in a large pot over medium heat. Add onions and cook until golden, about 10 minutes.
2. Add ginger-garlic paste, coriander powder, cumin powder, turmeric powder, and garam masala. Stir and cook for 1 minute.
3. Add the mutton cubes and stir to coat in the spices.
4. Add the chopped tomatoes and ground red chili and stir to combine.
5. Reduce the heat to low, cover the pot, and cook for 30 minutes, stirring occasionally.
6. Uncover the pot and cook for an additional 15 minutes, or until the mutton is cooked through.
7. Taste and adjust the seasoning with salt as necessary.
8. Serve the curry with chopped fresh cilantro on top.

Nutrition information:
Calories: 202 kcal,
Carbohydrates: 6 g,
Protein: 18 g,
Fat: 11 g,
Saturated Fat: 5 g,
Cholesterol: 57 mg,
Sodium: 125 mg,
Potassium: 377 mg,
Fiber: 2 g,
Sugar: 2 g,
Vitamin A: 843 IU,
Vitamin C: 13 mg,
Calcium: 92 mg,
Iron: 3 mg.

44. Lahori Chicken Handi

Lahori Chicken Handi is a flavorful and hearty Pakistani dish made up of marinated chicken, warm spices, and creamy yogurt sauce.

Serving: Serves 4.
Preparation Time: 20 minutes
Ready Time: 35 minutes

Ingredients:
- 4 boneless, skinless chicken breasts, cubed
- 1 cup plain yogurt
- 2 tablespoons garlic paste
- 2 tablespoons ginger paste
- 2 tablespoons garam masala
- Salt, to taste
- 2 tablespoons olive oil
- 1 onion, diced
- 2 tomatoes, diced
- 1 jalapeno pepper, chopped
- 1/2 cup fresh cilantro, chopped
- 2 green chilis, chopped

Instructions:
1. In a large bowl, mix together the yogurt, garlic paste, ginger paste, garam masala, and salt. Add the chicken cubes and mix until everything is evenly coated. Marinate in the refrigerator for at least 20 minutes.
2. Heat the olive oil in a heavy-bottomed pot over medium-high heat. Add the onion and cook until lightly browned, about 5 minutes.
3. Add the tomatoes, jalapeno pepper, cilantro, and green chilis. Cook for another 5 minutes.
4. Add the marinated chicken and stir to combine. Reduce heat to low and cook for 20 minutes, stirring occasionally.
5. Serve hot with naan or steamed rice.

Nutrition information:
Calories: 396 kcal, Carbohydrates: 9 g, Protein: 32 g, Fat: 24 g, Saturated Fat: 6 g, Cholesterol: 96 mg, Sodium: 277 mg, Potassium: 677 mg, Fiber: 3 g, Sugar: 5 g, Vitamin A: 541 IU, Vitamin C: 17 mg, Calcium: 105 mg, Iron: 2 mg

45. Lahori Kebab Paratha

Lahori Kebab Paratha is a traditional Pakistani flatbread filled with spiced beef and served for breakfast or brunch. It is a popular snack and street food in Lahore.

Serving: 4
Preparation Time: 15 minutes
Ready Time: 40 minutes

Ingredients:
- 2 cups all-purpose flour
- 1 teaspoon salt
- 2 tablespoons vegetable oil
- 1 cup warm water
- 1 pound ground beef
- 1/2 teaspoon Kashmiri red chili powder
- 1/2 teaspoon turmeric
- 1 teaspoon coriander powder
- 1 teaspoon garam masala
- 1 tablespoon fresh ginger, minced
- 2 tablespoons fresh cilantro leaves, chopped
- Salt, to taste

Instructions:
1. In a bowl, mix together the flour and salt, and then stir in the oil. Gradually add the warm water until the dough comes together. Knead for 5-7 minutes, until it is elastic and soft. Cover and set aside for at least 15 minutes.
2. In a large skillet, heat the beef over medium heat and cook until it is browned. Add the chili powder, turmeric, coriander powder, garam masala, ginger, cilantro, and salt, and stir to combine. Cook for 5-7 minutes, or until the beef is fully cooked.
3. Divide the dough into 4 equal pieces. On a lightly floured work surface, roll the dough out into circles about 18-20cm (7-8 inches) in diameter.
4. To assemble the parathas, spoon the cooked beef mixture onto one side of the dough circles, then fold over, pressing the edges to seal.
5. Heat a skillet over medium heat and place the paratha onto the skillet. Cook for about 5 minutes, or until the underside is golden brown. Flip over and cook for an additional 5 minutes.
6. Serve hot with yogurt and chutney.

Nutrition information:
Each serving of Lahori Kebab Paratha contains 466 calories, 13g fat, 63g carbohydrates, and 22g protein.

46. Lahori Gajar Halwa

Lahori Gajar Halwa is a traditional Punjabi dessert made of grated carrots, nuts, milk, and sugar, and spiced with cardamom and cinnamon.
Serving: 4 servings
Preparation time: 20 minutes
Ready time: 50 minutes

Ingredients:
• 4 cups carrots, grated
• 3 cups of milk
• 1/2 cup ghee
• 1 cup sugar
• 2 tablespoons raisins
• 2 tablespoons chopped nuts of your choice (almonds, cashews, or pistachios)
• 1/2 teaspoon ground cardamom
• 1/2 teaspoon ground cinnamon

Instructions:
1. Grate carrots and set aside.
2. Heat ghee in a large saucepan over medium heat and add the grated carrots. Fry for 8-10 minutes until lightly browned.
3. Add the milk and cook until the carrots are fully cooked and the milk has been absorbed.
4. Add the sugar, raisins, nuts, cardamom, and cinnamon. Mix well.
5. Continue to cook for 20-30 minutes until the halwa is thick and all the liquid is absorbed.
6. Serve hot or warm.

Nutrition information:
• Calories: 180 per serving
• Fat: 7 g per serving
• Protein: 2 g per serving

- Carbs: 27 g per serving

47. Lahori Chicken Kofta

Lahori Chicken Kofta is a traditional Pakistani dish, cooked with distinct and bold flavors. It features chicken koftas - spiced and shallow fried chicken balls - served in a smooth, aromatic sauce.
Serving: 4-6
Preparation time: 15 minutes
Ready time: 40 minutes

Ingredients:
- 500g chicken mince
- 2 small onions, grated
- 2 tbsp fresh coriander, chopped
- 1 cup breadcrumbs
- 3 tbsp olive oil
- 2 cloves garlic, minced
- 1 tbsp fresh ginger, minced
- 3 green chilies, finely chopped
- 1 tsp cumin powder
- 1 tsp garam masala
- 2 cups chicken stock
- 2 large tomatoes, pureed
- 1 tsp red chili powder
- 2 tablespoons yogurt
- 2 tablespoons cream
- Salt, to taste

Instructions:
1. In a bowl, mix together the chicken mince, grated onion, coriander, breadcrumbs, olive oil, garlic, ginger, chilies, cumin powder and garam masala. Shape into small balls.
2. Heat oil in a large pan over medium heat. Add the koftas and fry until golden brown. Drain and set aside.
3. In the same pan, add the chicken stock, tomato puree, red chilli powder, yogurt and cream. Simmer for 4-5 minutes over medium heat.

4. Add the koftas to the sauce and cook for 10-15 minutes, stirring occasionally.

5. Season with salt to taste and serve hot with steamed rice or naan.

Nutrition information: Each serving of Lahori Chicken Koftas has 349 Calories, 15.5 grams of Fat, 24.2 grams of Protein and 17.8 grams of Carbohydrates.

48. Lahori Vegetable Biryani

Lahori Vegetable Biryani is a delicious Indian dish prepared with long-grain basmati rice, a range of colorful vegetables, and an aromatic blend of spices.

Serving: 4-5

Preparation Time: 25 minutes

Ready Time: 50 minutes

Ingredients:
- 2 tsp vegetable oil
- 1 small onion, finely sliced
- 1-2 cloves garlic, finely chopped
- 1-2 cm fresh ginger, finely grated
- ½ cup diced tomato
- 2-3 tsp of ground spices (of your choice like cumin, coriander, garam masala, turmeric)
- ½ cup of mixed vegetables of your choice (carrot, capsicum, green beans, peas, cauliflower etc)
- 1 ½ cup basmati rice
- 2 cups vegetable stock
- ½ tsp salt
- 3-4 tbsp of freshly chopped cilantro (coriander leaves)

Instructions:
1. Heat oil in a heavy bottomed pan or pot over a medium heat.
2. Add the finely sliced onion and fry until golden brown.
3. Add the garlic and ginger and fry for one minute.
4. Add the diced tomato and cook for 2 minutes then add the spices and fry for 1 minute.

5. Add the mixed vegetables and fry for 2-3 minutes.
6. Add the basmati rice and fry for 1 minute.
7. Add the vegetable stock and salt and stir the mix.
8. Cover and cook for 25 minutes- until the rice is cooked and all the liquid is absorbed.
9. Turn off the heat and stir in the freshly chopped cilantro (coriander leaves).
10. Serve hot with raita or salad of your choice.

Nutrition information: Calories: 347, Fat: 8.7g, Carbohydrates: 56.8g, Protein: 7.7g, Fiber: 3.6g, Sugar: 5.2g.

49. Lahori Aloo Paratha

Lahori Aloo Paratha is a scrumptious Pakistani dish which is made up of potatoes and spices stuffed in a flatbread.
Serving: 4
Preparation time: 25 minutes
Ready Time: 40 minutes

Ingredients:
- 4 pieces of flatbread
- 4 potatoes, boiled and mashed
- 2 ½ teaspoon of red chili powder
- 1 teaspoon of coriander powder
- 1 teaspoon of cumin powder
- 1 teaspoon grated ginger
- 2 tablespoons of oil
- 1 teaspoon garam masala
-Salt to taste

Instructions:

1. Mix mashed potatoes with chili powder, coriander powder, cumin powder, grated ginger, and garam masala along with salt.
2. Take a flatbread and spread the potato mixture on one half of it.
3. Fold the other half of the flatbread over the one which has the potato mixture.

4. Heat oil in a pan and put the paratha in it.

5. Fry the paratha on both sides until it is golden brown.

6. Serve the Lahori Aloo Paratha with tamarind chutney or yogurt.

Nutrition information: (per serving)
Calories: 344 kcal
Carbohydrates: 48.8 g
Fat: 9.9 g
Protein: 6.3 g
Sodium: 149.6 mg
Potassium: 477.3 mg

50. Lahori Baingan Bharta

Lahori Baingan Bharta is a deliciously spicy eggplant curry originating from Lahore, Pakistan. It is a popular North Indian main dish and is prepared in Punjabi households.
Serving: 4-6 people
Preparation Time: 15 minutes
Ready Time: 35 minutes

Ingredients:
- 4 medium eggplants
- 2 tablespoons of ghee
- 1 onion, chopped
- 1 tablespoon of minced garlic
- 1 teaspoon of grated ginger
- 2 green chilies, chopped
- 3 tomatoes, chopped
- 1 tablespoon of coriander powder
- Salt, to taste
- 1 teaspoon of garam masala
- 2 tablespoons of chopped coriander leaves
- 2 tablespoons of ghee, for garnish

Instructions:
1. Heat the ghee in a large wok or saucepan over medium-high heat.
2. Add the chopped onion and sauté until it is golden-brown.

3. Add the garlic, ginger, and green chilies and sauté for a few more minutes.
4. Add the chopped tomatoes and cook until they are soft and mushy.
5. Add the eggplants and cook for 10 minutes, stirring occasionally.
6. Add the coriander powder and salt and mix together thoroughly.
7. Cover and cook the eggplant mixture for 15 minutes, stirring occasionally.
8. Remove from heat and stir in the garam masala and chopped coriander leaves.
9. Transfer the bharta to a plate and garnish with the remaining ghee.

Nutrition information:
Calories: 190
Fat: 13g
Carbohydrates: 19g
Protein: 4g
Fiber: 5g

51. Lahori Chicken Paratha Roll

Lahori Chicken Paratha Roll is a delicious and traditional dish of Pakistani cuisine. It is very quick and easy to make, full of flavor, and guaranteed to tantalize your taste buds. This dish takes advantage of the amazing flavors and spices of Pakistani cuisine, and is sure to become a favorite in your household.
Serving: 4-6 servings
Preparation time: 15 mins
Ready time: 50-60 mins

Ingredients:
-3 tablespoons vegetable oil
-700 grams boneless chicken tenders, cubed
-2 tablespoons garlic and ginger paste
-2 tablespoons chili paste
-1 teaspoon coriander powder
-2 teaspoons chili powder
-1 teaspoon garam masala
-1/2 cup yogurt

-4 paratha
-1 onion, sliced
-2 tomatoes, sliced

Instructions:
1. Heat the oil in a pan over medium heat.
2. Add the chicken cubes and garlic and ginger paste and cook for 5 minutes until the chicken is just cooked.
3. Add the chili paste, coriander powder, chili powder, and garam masala. Mix to combine.
4. Lower the heat to low, and add the yogurt. Mix and cook for 5 minutes until the chicken is lightly browned and stir occasionally.
5. Place one paratha on a plate. Put some of the chicken mixture in the center.
6. Top with onion and tomato slices.
7. Roll up the paratha and secure with a toothpick.
8. Heat a large skillet over medium-high heat.
9. Place the paratha roll in the skillet and cook for 3 minutes, reduce the heat to medium and cook for 8-10 minutes, flipping occasionally until the paratha roll is nice and crispy.

Nutrition information:
Calories: 433, Total fat: 24 grams, Saturated fat: 4 grams, Total carbohydrates: 17 grams, Protein: 34 grams, Cholesterol: 94 milligrams, Sodium: 434 milligrams, Fiber: 3 grams.

52. Lahori Dum Pukht Biryani

Lahori Dum Pukht Biryani is an aromatic and flavorful rice dish from the streets of Lahore, Pakistan. It is cooked in a sealed pot to bring out its unique aroma and irresistible flavor. The dish is prepared with basmati rice and succulent pieces of chicken all marinated in a yoghurt-based marinade with special Pakistani spices and herbs.
Serving: 6
Preparation Time: 15 minutes
Ready Time: 45 minutes

Ingredients:

- 1 kg basmati rice
- 500g chicken, cut into small pieces
- 2 cups plain yogurt
- 2 large onions, finely chopped
- 5 cloves garlic, minced
- 4 tablespoons vegetable oil
- 2 tablespoons ginger paste
- 2 tablespoons garam masala powder
- 1 teaspoon cumin powder
- 1 teaspoon red chilli powder
- 1 teaspoon turmeric powder
- 1 teaspoon garam masala powder
- 1 teaspoon freshly ground black pepper
- 2 cloves
- 1 bay leaf
- 2 blackCardamom
- 6 green chillies, chopped

Instructions:

1. In a large bowl, marinate the chicken pieces with yogurt, 1 tablespoon ginger paste, 1 teaspoon cumin powder, 1 teaspoon red chilli powder, 1 teaspoon turmeric powder, 1 teaspoon garam masala powder and 1 teaspoon black pepper for at least 1 hour.

2. In a large pot over medium heat, heat the oil and add the onions and garlic. Saute until the onion is lightly browned — about 8 minutes.

3. Add the remaining ginger paste, garam masala powder, cumin powder, red chilli powder, turmeric powder, garam masala powder and black pepper. Stir for 1 minute.

4. Add the marinated chicken and stir for 4 minutes.

5. Add the basmati rice, cloves, bay leaf, black cardamom and green chillies. Stir for another minute.

6. Add 6 cups of water and bring to a boil.

7. Reduce heat to low and cover the pot. Simmer for 20 minutes.

8. Uncover the pot and fluff the rice gently with a fork. Cover the pot again and simmer for 10 more minutes.

9. Turn off the heat and let the dish rest for 5 minutes.

10. Serve the Lahori Dum Pukht Biryani with onions cubes, lemon wedges and a salad.

Nutrition information:

Calories: 420, Total fat: 9g, Saturated fat: 1.5g, Cholesterol: 78mg, Sodium: 300mg, Total carbohydrates: 61g, Dietary fiber: 3g, Sugar: 3g, Protein: 24g.

53. Lahori Palak Paneer

Lahori Palak Paneer is a popular North Indian dish, which is a rich combination of creamy spinach and soft cottage cheese. This preparation uses a simple set of spices to give it an unforgettable flavor.
Serving: 4-5
Preparation time: 15 minutes
Ready time: 45 minutes

Ingredients:
- 1/2 kg fresh spinach
- 100 gm paneer (cottage cheese) cubes
- 2 onions, chopped
- 2 tomatoes, chopped
- 1 teaspoon garlic, chopped
- 1 tablespoon ginger, chopped
- 3 green chillies, chopped
- 1 teaspoon coriander powder
- 1 teaspoon red chilli powder
- 1 teaspoon cumin powder
- 2 teaspoons garam masala
- 2 tablespoons oil
- Salt to taste

Instructions:
1. In a deep pan, heat oil.
2. Once the oil is hot, add onions, garlic, ginger and green chillies.
3. Cook for 2-3 minutes and then add chopped tomatoes.
4. Cook for 5 minutes till the tomatoes become tender.
5. Add coriander powder, red chilli powder, cumin powder and garam masala. Stir well.
6. Now add spinach and paneer cubes to the pan.
7. Cover the pan and cook for 15 minutes on medium heat.
8. Remove the lid and simmer for few minutes.

9. Add salt to taste and stir.
10. Serve hot with naan or tandoori roti.

Nutrition information:
Calories: 126
Fat: 9g
Carbohydrates: 8.7g
Protein: 4.3g

54. Lahori Chicken Tikka Biryani

Lahori Chicken Tikka Biryani is a delicious and flavorful Pakistani dish, made with marinated chicken, basmati rice, and onions. It has a rich and aromatic flavor that will have your guests wanting more.
Serving: 4
Preparation time: 20 minutes
Ready time: 40 minutes

Ingredients:
• 500 g boneless chicken pieces
• 2 tablespoons of ginger and garlic paste
• 1 onion, finely chopped
• 2 tablespoons oil
• 2 tablespoons yoghurt
• 2 teaspoons cumin powder
• 2 teaspoons garam masala
• 2 teaspoons chilli powder
• 2 teaspoons coriander powder
• Salt to taste
• 2 cups basmati rice, pre-soaked for 30 minutes
• 2 onions, thickly sliced
• 2 cardamom pods
• 4 cloves
• 4 black peppercorns
• 2 bay leaves
• 1 cinnamon stick
• 2 tablespoons ghee
• 1/2 cup fried onions

- 2 tablespoons chopped coriander
- 2 tablespoons chopped mint

Instructions:
1. Marinate the chicken pieces with the ginger–garlic paste, yoghurt, chilli powder, garam masala, coriander powder and salt. Leave to marinate for a minimum of 30 minutes.
2. Heat the oil in a large pan and sauté the chopped onion until golden brown. Add the marinated chicken and cook until the chicken has changed color.
3. Meanwhile in a separate pan, heat the ghee and sauté the sliced onions with the whole spices and the bay leaves until golden brown.
4. Add the pre-soaked basmati rice and fry for a few minutes.
5. Add 2 cups of water to the pan and bring to a boil.
6. Add the fried onions, chopped coriander and mint and then mix.
7. Place the chicken on top of the rice and cover with a lid.
8. Cook on low heat for 20 minutes until the rice and chicken are cooked through.
9. Serve hot with yogurt and chutney.

Nutrition information:
Calories: 451.5, Fat: 21.5g, Cholestrol: 116.5mg, Sodium: 624mg, Carbohydrates: 37.5g, Protein: 26.5g, Sugar: 4.5g

55. Lahori Daal Makhani

Lahori Daal Makhani is a fragrant and delicious Indian dish that is made with a combination of black lentils, split moong beans, butter and cream.
Serving: 4-6
Preparation time: 15 minutes
Ready time: 45 minutes

Ingredients:
- 2 cups black lentils (daal)
- 1 cup split moong beans (mung beans)
- 2 tablespoons vegetable oil
- 2 teaspoons cumin seeds
- 2 bay leaves

- 1 large onion, minced
- 3 cloves garlic, minced
- 3 tablespoons grated ginger
- 1 teaspoon turmeric
- 1 teaspoon cayenne pepper
- 1 teaspoon garam masala
- 4 tablespoons butter
- 1 (14.5 ounce) can diced tomatoes
- 2 cups water
- 1/2 cup heavy cream
- Salt, to taste

Instructions:

1. Rinse the lentils and mung beans in a fine sieve, then drain them and set aside.
2. Heat oil in a large pot over medium-high heat. Add the cumin seeds and bay leaves and cook for 1 minute.
3. Add the onion, garlic, and ginger to the pot and cook, stirring, until the onion is softened.
4. Add the turmeric, cayenne pepper, and garam masala and mix to combine.
5. Add the butter, tomatoes, and water. Bring to a boil then reduce the heat to simmer.
6. Add the lentils and mung beans and continue to simmer, covered, for 25-30 minutes, stirring occasionally.
7. Add the cream and stir to combine. Simmer for an additional 10 minutes, stirring occasionally.
8. Season with salt, to taste.

Nutrition information:
Calories: 305, Total Fat: 12g, Saturated Fat: 6g, Cholesterol: 29mg, Sodium: 535mg, Carbohydrates: 35g, Fiber: 8g, Protein: 11g.

56. Lahori Mutton Paya

Lahori Mutton Paya is a hearty and flavorful mutton dish that originates from Pakistan and is a much loved food in the region.
Serving: 4

Preparation Time: 30 mins
Ready Time: 1 hour

Ingredients:
- 2 kg mutton (leg cut)
- 8 cups water
- 4 tbsp ginger garlic paste
- 1 ½ cups chopped onions
- Juice of 1 lime
- 5 tbsp oil
- 8 cloves
- 4 cinnamon sticks
- 4 cardamom pods
- 6 black peppercorns
- 2 black cardamom pods
- 2 tsp garam masala
- 2 tsp cumin powder
- 1 tsp red chilli powder
- Salt to taste

Instructions:
1. Place the mutton and water in a large pot and bring to a boil. Reduce heat to low and simmer for 45 mins, skimming off any fat that rises to the top.
2. In a separate pan, heat the oil and add in the onions, ginger garlic paste, cloves, cinnamon sticks, cardamom pods, black peppercorns, and black cardamom pods. Saute until the onions are golden brown.
3. Add the onion mixture into the boiling mutton and season with garam masala, cumin powder, red chilli powder, and salt. Mix and simmer for another 15 mins.
4. Add the lime juice and simmer for a few more minutes, or until the mutton is tender and the gravy is thick and flavorful.

Nutrition information:
Calories: 550 kcal, Carbohydrates: 27g, Protein: 53g, Fat: 19g, Saturated Fat: 4g, Sodium: 824mg, Potassium: 1016mg, Fiber: 5g, Sugar: 6g, Vitamin A: 282IU, Calcium: 85mg, Iron: 3mg.

57. Lahori Bhuna Gosht

Lahori Bhuna Gosht is a Pakistani delicacy made with pieces of meat cooked in spices. As the name suggests, it originated in the city of Lahore. The flavor is rich and intense and is usually served with naan or other types of bread.

Serving: 4
Preparation Time: 10 minutes
Ready Time: 40 minutes

Ingredients:
– 1 kg. boneless lamb, cubed
– 6 tablespoons vegetable oil
– 1 large onion, sliced
– 1 tablespoon freshly grated ginger
– 5 cloves garlic, chopped
– 2 teaspoons cumin powder
– 2 teaspoons coriander powder
– 2 teaspoons red chili powder
– 2 tablespoons tomato puree
– Salt to taste

Instructions:
1. Heat the oil in a heavy-bottomed pan.
2. Add the sliced onions and sauté them until light golden.
3. Add the ginger and garlic and fry for a minute.
4. Add the cubed lamb and fry for 5 minutes.
5. Add the cumin powder, coriander powder, red chili powder, tomato puree, and salt. Stir to combine all the Ingredients and cook for 10 minutes, stirring occasionally.
6. Add 2-3 tablespoons of water and cover the pan with a lid. Simmer for 25-30 minutes until the lamb is cooked and the gravy is thick.
7. Serve hot with naan or other types of bread.

Nutrition information: Per Serving – Calories 375, Total Fat 18g (Saturated Fat 6g, Trans Fat 0g), Cholesterol 79mg, Sodium 282mg, Total Carbohydrate 20g (Dietary Fibre 5g, Sugars 9g), Protein 32g.

58. Lahori Aloo Palak

Lahori Aloo Palak is a classic Pakistani dish that features potatoes and spinach cooked together in a rich, tomato-based sauce. This fragrant and delicious dish is a perfect meal for any night of the week!
Serving: 4
Preparation time: 15 minutes
Ready time: 30 minutes

Ingredients:
-3 medium-sized potatoes, peeled and diced
-4 cups of fresh spinach leaves
-1/2 cup diced onions
-3 cloves of garlic, minced
-1 teaspoon of cumin powder
-1 teaspoon of coriander powder
-1 teaspoon of red chili powder
-1/2 teaspoon of turmeric powder
-2 tablespoons of tomato paste
-4 tablespoons of vegetable oil
-Salt and pepper to taste

Instructions:
1. Heat the oil in a large pan over medium heat.
2. Add the onions and garlic and sauté until the onions are softened and fragrant, about 5 minutes.
3. Add the potatoes and stir to combine, then reduce the heat to low and cover the pan. Let the potatoes cook for about 10 minutes, stirring occasionally.
4. Add the spinach leaves, cumin powder, coriander powder, red chili powder, turmeric powder, and tomato paste. Raise the heat to medium-high and stir to combine.
5. Cover the pan and let the spinach and potato mixture cook for 10 minutes, stirring occasionally.
6. When the potatoes are cooked through and the spinach has wilted, season with salt and pepper to taste.
7. Serve the Lahori Aloo Palak warm, with a side of naan or rice if desired. Enjoy!

Nutrition information:

Serving size: 1/4 of the dish
Calories: 250
Fat: 19 g
Carbohydrates: 19 g
Protein: 4 g

59. Lahori Paneer Butter Masala

Lahori Paneer Butter Masala is a rich and creamy North Indian dish. It is prepared from paneer marinated in spices and cooked in a buttery gravy.
Serving: Serves 4
Preparation Time: 10 mins
Ready Time: 30 mins

Ingredients:
- Paneer, 250g
- Tomatoes, 2
- Onions, 2
- Ginger-Garlic Paste, 1 tsp
- Coriander Powder, 1 tsp
- Chilli Powder, 1 tsp
- Turmeric Powder, ½ tsp
- Cumin Powder, 1 tsp
- Salt, to taste
- Coriander Leaves, 1 tbsp (chopped)
- Garam Masala, ½ tsp
- Butter, 2 tbsp
- Milk, 2 cups

Instructions:
1. Start by tenderizing the paneer blocks with a rolling pin or mallet.
2. Blitz the tomatoes, onions, ginger-garlic paste, coriander powder, chili powder, turmeric powder, cumin powder and salt in a food processor to make a paste.
3. Heat butter in a pan over medium flame.
4. Once the butter melts, add the paste and mix until combined.
5. Cook the paste for around 8-10 minutes, stirring constantly.
6. Add the paneer and mix to coat the paneer with the spices and butter.

7. Pour in the milk and bring the curry to a boil.
8. Simmer for 10 minutes and add the garam masala.
9. Let the curry cook for another 5 minutes for the flavors to combine.
10. Garnish with chopped coriander leaves and serve hot.

Nutrition information:
Calories: 262 kcal; Fat: 17.1g; Protein: 17.2g; Carbohydrates:10.2g;
Sodium: 0.3g; Fiber: 2.2g

60. Lahori Beef Curry

Lahori Beef Curry is a delicious curry dish that originates from the city of
Lahore in Pakistan. It is made with a variety of spices and beef cut into
small cubes, and is often served with rice or naan.
Serving: 4
Preparation time: 10 minutes
Ready time: 40 minutes

Ingredients:
- 1-pound beef, cut into cubes
- 1 tablespoon vegetable oil
- 1 teaspoon coriander powder
- 1 teaspoon cumin powder
- 1 teaspoon garam masala
- 2-3 fresh tomatoes, chopped
- 2 cloves garlic, minced
- 1 teaspoon fresh ginger, grated
- ½ teaspoon red chili powder
- 2 tablespoons fresh cilantro, chopped
- 1 cup hot water
- Salt to taste

Instructions:
1. Heat the oil in a large pot over medium-high heat.
2. Add the beef cubes to the pot and cook for 3-4 minutes until lightly
browned.
3. Add the coriander, cumin, garam masala, tomatoes, garlic, ginger, and
chili powder to the pot. Stir to combine.

4. Cook for 5-7 minutes, stirring occasionally, until the beef is cooked through.
5. Add the cilantro, hot water, and salt. Bring to a boil, then reduce the heat to low and simmer for 25-30 minutes.

Nutrition information:
Calories: 128
Total Fat: 6.7 g
Cholesterol: 29.9 mg
Sodium: 174 mg
Carbohydrates: 2.6 g
Protein: 14.1 g

61. Lahori Chicken Jalfrezi

Lahori Chicken Jalfrezi is a popular Pakistani dish. It is a spicy curry prepared with chicken, bell peppers, and other spices.
Serving: 4
Preparation Time: 15 minutes
Ready Time: 45 minutes

Ingredients:
- 4 boneless chicken breasts
- 1 onion, finely chopped
- 1 teaspoon ginger paste
- 1 teaspoon garlic paste
- 1 teaspoon cumin powder
- 1 teaspoon coriander powder
- ¼ teaspoon red chilli powder
- 1 tablespoon tomato paste
- 1 bell pepper, chopped
- 1 teaspoon garam masala
- Salt to taste
- 2 tablespoons oil

Instructions:
1. Heat oil in a large pan over medium heat.
2. Add the onion and sauté until golden brown.

3.   Stir in the ginger & garlic paste, cumin powder, coriander powder, red chilli powder, and tomato paste and sauté for 1 minute.
4.   Add the chicken and bell pepper and cook until the chicken is lightly browned.
5.   Add 4 tablespoons of water, cover the pan, and simmer for 25 minutes.
6.   Uncover the pan and stir in the garam masala and salt to taste.
7.   Simmer for an additional 10 minutes or until the chicken is cooked through.
8.   Serve hot.

Nutrition information: Calories: 294, Protein: 31.2g, Fat: 14.7g, Carbohydrates: 5g, Fiber: 1.3g, Sugar: 1.3g

62. Lahori Achari Chicken

Lahori Achari Chicken is a deliciously spiced, tangy and flavourful curry made with boneless chicken, yogurt and an aromatic masala.
Serving: 4
Preparation Time: 10 minutes
Ready Time: 40 minutes

Ingredients:
• 500 gms boneless chicken
• 1 cup yogurt
• 2 onions chopped
• 2 tbsp ginger garlic paste
• 2 tsp red chili powder
• ½ tsp garam masala
• 4 green chillies chopped
• 2 tomatoes chopped
• ¼ cup oil
• 2 tsp cumin seeds
• 1.5 tsp coriander powder
• 1.5 tsp fennel powder
• 1.5 tsp fenugreek powder
• 1.5 tsp Kashmiri red chilli powder
• Salt to taste

Instructions:
1. Heat oil in a pot; add cumin seeds and let them crackle.
2. Add onions and cook until they are brown.
3. Add ginger garlic paste, red chili powder, garam masala, green chilli chopped, and cook for 1-2 minutes.
4. Add chicken and cook till the chicken is done.
5. Add yogurt and mix well.
6. Add coriander powder, fennel powder, fenugreek powder, Kashmiri red chilli powder and salt to taste.
7. Add tomatoes and cook until tomatoes are soft.
8. Add 1 cup water and bring the curry to a boil.
9. Simmer the curry for 10-15 minutes until it is cooked and the oil starts to separate.
10. Finally, garnish with coriander leaves and serve hot.

Nutrition information:
Calories: 305, Total Fat: 16.2g, Cholesterol: 73mg, Sodium: 290mg, Total Carbohydrates: 10.6g Protein: 27.2g

63. Lahori Chutney

Lahori Chutney is a vibrant and flavorful condiment that originates from Lahore, Pakistan. It is an amazing blend of flavors, combining a variety of spices and ingedients.
Serving: Makes approx. one cup
Preparation time: 10 minutes
Ready time: 20 minutes

Ingredients:
• 2 cups fresh coriander
• 1 medium onion, diced
• 1 small green chili
• 2 garlic cloves, minced
• 1 tsp cumin seeds
• A pinch of salt
• 2-3 tbsp lemon juice
• 2 tbsp olive oil

• 1/4 tsp ground black pepper

Instructions:
1. In a blender or food processor, combine the coriander, onion, green chili, garlic, and cumin seeds and blend until a smooth paste is formed.
2. Add the salt, lemon juice, olive oil, and black pepper and blend for a few seconds to combine.
3. Transfer to a bowl and cover. Refrigerate for 10 minutes.
4. Serve the chutney chilled or at room temperature.

Nutrition information: Per 1/4 cup serving, this chutney contains approximately 40 calories, 4g fat, 2g carbohydrates, 1g protein, and 1g dietary fiber.

64. Lahori Baingan Ka Bharta

Lahori Baingan Ka Bharta is a popular and traditional dish native to the Punjab region of Pakistan and Northern India. It is an easy to make recipe that is healthy and nutritious.
Serving: 4
Preparation Time: 10 Mins
Ready Time: 20 Mins

Ingredients:
- 4 medium eggplants
- 2 tablespoons oil
- 1 teaspoon cumin seeds
- 1 large onion (diced)
- 2 green chillies (chopped)
- 2 teaspoons garlic paste
- 2 teaspoons ginger paste
- 1 teaspoon chilli powder
- 2 tomatoes (diced)
- 2 tablespoons coriander
- Salt (to taste)

Instructions:
1. Preheat the oven to 350 degrees Fahrenheit.

2. Place the eggplants in the oven and bake for 10 minutes.
3. Remove the eggplants and allow to cool.
4. Peel and mash the eggplants with a fork or potato masher.
5. Heat a large skillet over medium heat and add the oil.
6. Once the oil is hot, add the cumin seeds.
7. Once the cumin seeds start to crackle, add the onions and green chillies. Fry until the onions are golden brown.
8. Add the garlic and ginger paste and fry for 2 minutes.
9. Add the chilli powder, tomatoes and eggplant mash.
10. Stir to combine and cook for 5 minutes until the vegetables are cooked through.
11. Add the coriander and salt (to taste).
12. Serve hot with your favourite roti or naan bread.

Nutrition information:
Calories- 156 kcal
Protein- 4.4 g
Carbs- 19.6 g
Fats- 11.1 g
Fiber- 7.4 g

65. Lahori Mutton Stew

Lahori Mutton Stew is a spicy and savory mutton stew traditionally cooked in Pakistani and Indian Cuisine.
Serving: 6-8
Preparation time: 10 minutes
Ready time: 1 hour

Ingredients:
• 2lbs of cubed mutton
• 2 tablespoons of kosher salt
• 2 teaspoons of cumin seeds
• 1 tablespoon of garam masala
• 1 teaspoon of red chili powder
• 1 teaspoon of coriander powder
• 1 teaspoon of turmeric powder
• 1 chopped onion

- 2 cloves of garlic
- 1 inch of grated ginger
- 1 diced tomato
- 2 tablespoons of cooking oil
- 3 cups of water

Instructions:
1. Heat a large pot over medium heat.
2. Add the cooking oil to the pot. Once the oil is hot, add the cumin seeds and wait until they start to splutter.
3. Add the chopped onion, garlic, and ginger and stir fry until the onions have softened.
4. Add the diced tomatoes and cook until they start to break down.
5. Add the cubed mutton and stir to combine with the onions, garlic and ginger.
6. Add the kosher salt, garam masala, red chili powder, coriander powder, and turmeric powder and stir to combine.
7. Add 3 cups of water and bring to a boil.
8. Reduce the heat to medium-low and let the stew simmer for 45 minutes, stirring occasionally, until the mutton is tender and the stew has thickened.
9. Serve with steamed basmati rice or naan bread.

Nutrition information:
Calories: 293
Fat: 9.6g
Carbohydrates: 6.3g
Protein: 39.9g

66. Lahori Kadhi Pakora

Lahori Kadhi Pakora is a dish from the city of Lahore in Pakistan. This dish is a zesty combination of dumplings called pakoras, in a thick tangy yogurt-based curry.
Serving: 4
Preparation Time: 15 minutes
Ready Time: 45 minutes

Ingredients:
- Yogurt: 1 kg
- Besan (gram flour): ½ cup
- Green chilies: 4-5, finely chopped
- Turmeric: ½ teaspoon
- Red chili powder: 1 teaspoon
- Salt: To taste
- Oil: To fry

Instructions:
1. In a large bowl, add yogurt, besan, green chilies, turmeric, red chili powder, and salt. Mix all the Ingredients together and make a smooth batter.
2. Heat oil in a pan for deep frying. Take small portions of the prepared batter and shape into small pakoras.
3. Carefully drop the pakoras in hot oil and fry until golden and crisp. Remove from the pan and place onto a paper towel lined plate to absorb excess oil.
4. In a saucepan heat 2 tablespoons of oil and add 1 teaspoon of cumin. Fry for a few seconds and then add the prepared pakoras.
5. Fry the pakoras in the oil for a few minutes until golden and then pour the prepared yogurt curry into the pan.
6. Let the curry simmer for 15-20 minutes until thick and creamy.
7. Serve Lahori Kadhi Pakora with steamed Basmati rice.

Nutrition information: Calories: 400, Fat: 11g, Protein: 16g, Fiber: 5g

67. Lahori Chicken Changezi

Lahori Chicken Changezi is a classic Pakistani dish, featuring succulent chicken cooked in a spicy, tangy tomato-based masala accompanied with onions and peppers. This classic dish is sure to satisfy any palate.
Serving: Serves 4
Preparation time: 20 minutes
Ready time: 45 minutes

Ingredients:

- 1 Tbsp vegetable oil
- 1 onion, finely sliced
- 2 green peppers, chopped
- 2 cloves garlic, finely chopped
- 2 cm piece of ginger, finely chopped
- 4 chicken breasts, cubed
- 2 medium-sized tomatoes, sliced
- 1 tsp garam masala
- 1 tsp coriander powder
- 1 tsp cumin powder
- Fresh coriander, to garnish

Instructions:
1. Heat the oil in a large skillet or wok over medium-high heat.
2. Add the onions, peppers, garlic, and ginger and stir-fry until the vegetables are softened.
3. Add the chicken and stir-fry until the chicken is no longer pink.
4. Add the tomatoes, garam masala, coriander powder, and cumin powder and stir-fry for another 5 minutes.
5. Reduce the heat to low and simmer for 30 minutes.
6. Garnish with fresh coriander and serve.

Nutrition information
Per serving (includes vegetables and does not include garnish):
- Calories: 257
- Protein: 35g
- Carbohydrates: 12g
- Fat: 8g
- Fiber: 2g
- Sodium: 140mg

68. Lahori Mix Daal

Lahori mix daal is a traditional Pakistani dish composed of spiced lentils and pulses. It has a rich and flavorful taste that can be enjoyed as a side dish or eaten as a main meal. This simple recipe is full of aromatic spices and is sure to please the whole family.
Serving: 4

Preparation Time: 10 minutes
Ready Time: 60 minutes

Ingredients:
- 1 cup mixed daal
- 2 tablespoons oil
- 1 teaspoon cumin seeds
- 2 cloves garlic, finely chopped
- 1 onion, chopped
- 2 tablespoons fresh coriander, chopped
- 2 tablespoons fresh mint, chopped
- 2 tablespoons ginger, finely chopped
- 2 green chillies, finely chopped
- 1 teaspoon chilli powder
- Salt, to taste
- 1 teaspoon turmeric
- 1 teaspoon garam masala
- 2 cups water

Instructions:
1. Heat the oil in a large pot over medium heat.
2. Add the cumin seeds and garlic and stir for 1 minute.
3. Add the onion, coriander, mint, ginger and green chillies and fry for 3 minutes.
4. Add the chilli powder, salt, turmeric and garam masala and fry for a further 1 minute.
5. Add the daal and fry for 5 minutes.
6. Add the water and bring to the boil. Reduce the heat and simmer for 40 minutes, or until the daal is cooked.
7. Serve hot.

Nutrition information: An approximate nutritional analysis for one serving of Lahori mix daal is as follows: Calories: 120, Total Fat: 4 g, Cholesterol: 0 mg, Sodium: 64 mg, Total Carbohydrate: 15 g, Protein: 6 g.

69. Lahori Peshawari Chicken Karahi

Lahori Peshawari Chicken Karahi is a delicious and flavorful Pakistani dish from the Lahori region. This dish is a delightful blend of aromatic spices and flavorful chicken that is cooked in a Karahi or wok. It is perfect for family meals, potlucks, or any special occasions.

Serving: Serves 4

Preparation Time: 30 minutes

Ready Time: 1 hour

Ingredients:
-500g boneless chicken, cut into cubes
-3-4 tablespoons Peshawari Karahi Masala
-2 tablespoons garlic paste
-1 tablespoon ginger paste
-3-4 tablespoons yogurt
-2 tablespoons cooking oil
-2 tablespoons lemon juice
-2 tablespoons crushed coriander
-1 teaspoon cumin powder
-1 teaspoon red chili powder
-Salt to taste

Instructions:
1. In a bowl, combine the chicken, garlic paste, ginger paste, yogurt, Karahi Masala, lemon juice, coriander, cumin powder, and red chili powder.
2. Mix these Ingredients together and add salt to taste. Let the chicken marinate for 30 minutes.
3. Heat the oil in the Karahi or wok on medium-high heat.
4. Add the marinated chicken and cook for 10-15 minutes or until the chicken is completely cooked.
5. When the chicken is cooked, reduce the flame to low and simmer the chicken for 5 minutes.
6. Garnish with crushed coriander and serve hot.

Nutrition information:
Calories: 256 Kcal, Carbohydrates: 8g, Protein: 27g, Fat: 8g, Saturated Fat: 2g, Trans Fat: 0g, Cholesterol: 43mg, Sodium: 641mg, Potassium: 508mg, Fiber: 1g, Sugar: 2g, Vitamin A: 147IU, Vitamin C: 13mg, Calcium: 74mg, Iron: 2mg.

70. Lahori Aloo Gobi

Lahori Aloo Gobi is an incredibly flavorful, vegan Punjabi dish full of potatoes, cauliflower, tomatoes, and spices. It's an easy one-pot meal full of Indian flavors that are sure to please even the pickiest of eaters.
Serving: 4
Preparation Time: 10 minutes
Ready Time: 30 minutes

Ingredients:
- 2 tablespoons of oil
- 2 teaspoons of cumin seeds
- 2 potatoes, peeled and cut into cubes
- 1 onion, diced
- 1 teaspoon of garlic, minced
- 2 teaspoons of ginger, minced
- 1 teaspoon of coriander powder
- 1 teaspoon of cumin powder
- 1 teaspoon of garam masala
- 1/2 teaspoon of turmeric powder
- 1 teaspoon of red chili powder
- 2 cups of cauliflower florets
- 2 tomatoes, chopped
- 1 cup of water
- Salt to taste

Instructions:
1. Heat the oil in a pan over medium heat.
2. Add the cumin seeds and allow them to sizzle for a minute.
3. Add the potatoes and onions to the pan and cook for about 5 minutes.
4. Add the garlic, ginger, coriander powder, cumin powder, garam masala, red chili powder, and turmeric powder, and mix well.
5. Add the cauliflower, tomatoes, and water and bring to a boil.
6. Reduce the heat to low, cover the pan and simmer for 15-20 minutes until the potatoes and cauliflower are cooked through.
7. Add salt to taste.
8. Serve with hot chapatis or naan.

Nutrition information:
Calories: 241; Total Fat: 8.1g; Saturated Fat: 0.8g; Cholesterol: 0mg; Sodium: 157mg; Carbohydrates: 38.3g; Dietary Fiber: 6.6g; Sugar: 6.7g; Protein: 6.8g

71. Lahori Chicken Malai Boti

Lahori Chicken Malai Boti is a traditional Pakistani chicken dish. It is deliciously spiced and cooked in a unique combination of authentic spices and cream, resulting in an incredibly flavorful and succulent dish.
Serving: 4
Preparation Time: 10 minutes
Ready Time: 45 minutes

Ingredients:
• 2 lb boneless chicken thighs, cubed
• 2 tablespoons of vegetable oil
• 1 teaspoon of garlic paste
• 1 teaspoon of ginger paste
• 1 teaspoon of cumin powder
• ½ teaspoon of ground coriander
• ½ teaspoon of garam masala
• ½ teaspoon of red chili powder
• 1 cup of heavy cream
• Salt and black pepper to taste

Instructions:
1. In a bowl, combine chicken thighs, garlic paste, ginger paste, cumin powder, ground coriander, garam masala and red chili powder. Stir until Ingredients are combined.
2. Heat the oil in a large pan over high heat.
3. Add the chicken mixture and cook for 10 minutes, stirring occasionally.
4. Reduce the heat to medium and add the heavy cream. Simmer for 25 minutes, stirring occasionally.
5. Add salt and pepper to taste.
6. Serve hot with your favorite side dishes.

Nutrition information:
Calories: 443 kcal,
Carbohydrates: 4 g,
Proteins: 35 g,
Fats: 30 g

72. Lahori Baingan Masala

Lahori Baingan Masala' is an authentic, flavorful Indian curry made with roasted eggplant and rich, spicy tomato sauce. It's the perfect dish to enjoy with your family and friends.
Serving: Serves 4
Preparation time: 10 minutes
Ready time: 30 minutes

Ingredients:
- 2 tablespoons vegetable oil
- 2 medium-sized eggplants, cut into cubes
- 3 teaspoons garam masala
- 2 teaspoons cumin powder
- 3 medium tomatoes, chopped
- 2 cloves garlic, minced
- 1 teaspoon ginger, minced
- 1/2 teaspoon turmeric powder
- Salt and pepper to taste

Instructions:
1. Heat the oil in a large pan over medium heat.
2. Add the eggplant cubes and cook for about 10 minutes, stirring occasionally.
3. Add the garam masala, cumin, tomatoes, garlic, ginger, turmeric, salt and pepper. Stir to combine.
4. Reduce the heat and cook for about 20 minutes, stirring occasionally until the eggplant is cooked through and the sauce is thick and rich.
5. Serve the Lahori Baingan Masala hot with your favorite flatbreads or basmati rice.

Nutrition information: Per Serving: Calories: 94; Total Fat: 7g; Carbohydrates: 8g; Protein: 2g; Cholesterol: 0mg; Sodium: 42mg

73. Lahori Chicken Reshmi Kebab

Lahori Chicken Reshmi Kebab is a restaurant-style, Mughlai dish. It packs an intense flavour due to the mix of aromatic spices, which is balanced by the yoghurt marinade.
Serving: 5-6
Preparation Time: 10 mins
Ready Time: 45 mins

Ingredients:
• 500 gm chicken
• 2 large onions, finely chopped
• 2 large tomatoes, finely chopped
• 2-3 green chillies, finely chopped
• 2 teaspoon ginger garlic paste
• 2 tablespoon oil
• 5-6 tablespoons plain yoghurt
• 2 tablespoon fresh cream
• 1 teaspoon garam masala
• 2 tablespoons coriander leaves
• 1 teaspoon red chilli powder
• 2 teaspoon coriander powder
• 2 teaspoon cumin powder
• 1 teaspoon kasuri methi
• Salt to taste

Instructions:
1. In a deep bowl mix together the yoghurt, cream, garam masala, red chilli powder, coriander powder, cumin powder, kasuri methi and salt.
2. Add in the chicken and mix well to ensure all the pieces are completely coated with the marinade. Set aside for 30 minutes.
3. Heat oil in a pan. Add in the onions and sauté until golden brown.
4. Add in the tomatoes and green chillies and sauté for another couple of minutes.
5. Add in the ginger garlic paste and mix well.

6. Add the marinated chicken and cook for 10-15 minutes or until chicken is cooked through.
7. Add in the coriander leaves and mix well.
8. Transfer to a serving plate and garnish with coriander leaves.

Nutrition information:
Calories: 370 kcal, Fat: 22 g, Protein: 27 g, Carbohydrates: 9 g, Fiber: 2g, Sugar: 4g, Sodium: 250mg

74. Lahori Mutton Biryani

Lahori Mutton Biryani is a traditional Pakistani biryani which is known for its spicy and delicious flavor. It consists of layers of spiced mutton and basmati rice that are cooked with herbs and spices.
Serving: 4-5
Preparation Time: 20 Minutes
Ready Time: 45 Minutes

Ingredients:
• 500g mutton, cut into pieces
• 1.5 cups basmati rice
• 2 onions, sliced
• 4 green chillies, finely chopped
• 1 teaspoon garlic paste
• 1 teaspoon ginger paste
• 2 teaspoons red chilli powder
• 2 teaspoons coriander powder
• 1 teaspoon garam masala
• 1/2 cup yogurt
• 2 tablespoons oil
• 1/2 cup chopped fresh coriander
• Salt to taste

Instructions:
1. In a large bowl, combine the mutton and yogurt and mix well. Add the green chillies, garlic paste, ginger paste, red chilli powder, coriander powder, garam masala, and salt, and mix until evenly incorporated.

2. Heat oil in a large pan over medium heat. Add the onions and fry until golden brown. Add the marinated mutton and fry until the pieces are browned all over.

3. Add 1 cup of water, reduce the heat, and simmer for 20-25 minutes or until the mutton is cooked and tender.

4. Add the basmati rice and mix gently. Cover and cook for 15-20 minutes or until the rice is cooked and all the liquid has been absorbed.

5. Garnish with chopped fresh coriander and serve hot.

Nutrition information:

Calories: 364, Fat: 15.2g, Protein: 24.1g, Carbohydrates: 33.2g, Fiber: 2g, Sugar: 3.2g, Sodium: 107.4 mg, Cholesterol: 45 mg

75. Lahori Chicken Curry

A delicious chicken curry with bold flavours, Lahori Chicken Curry is a popular dish from Pakistan. It is perfect to serve with fluffy basmati rice for a wholesome dinner.

Serving: Serves 6
Preparation Time: 15 minutes
Ready Time: 45 minutes

Ingredients:
- 2 tablespoons vegetable oil
- 2 onions, chopped
- 1 teaspoon ground cumin
- 2 teaspoons ground coriander
- 3 cloves garlic, minced
- 300g boneless and skinless chicken, cut into cubes
- ½ teaspoon turmeric
- 1 teaspoon garam masala
- 2 tomatoes, finely chopped
- 200ml natural yoghurt
- 2 teaspoons freshly chopped coriander
- Salt to taste

Instructions:

1. Heat the oil in a pan over a medium heat. Add the onions and fry until golden and softened.
2. Stir in the cumin, coriander and garlic and fry for a few minutes.
3. Add the chicken cubes and fry until sealed and golden.
4. Add the turmeric and garam masala, stir together and fry for a few minutes.
5. Add the tomatoes and cook for a further 10 minutes.
6. Pour in the yoghurt and bring to the boil.
7. Reduce the heat to low and simmer for 20 minutes, stirring occasionally.
8. Garnish with the fresh coriander and season with salt to taste.

Nutrition information (per serve):
Calories: 192
Fat: 11.9g
Carbohydrates: 9.7g
Protein: 12.4g

76. Lahori Methi Chicken

This succulent Lahori Methi Chicken is a traditional Pakistani chicken curry recipe that will tantalize your taste buds with its lively flavors. This recipe features flavorful spices, dried fenugreek leaves, and tender chicken for a meal that's sure to please.
Serving: 4-6 people
Preparation time: 15 minutes
Ready time: 45 minutes

Ingredients:
• 2 lbs skinless chicken pieces
• 2 tablespoons canola oil
• 1 onion, chopped
• 2 cloves garlic, minced
• 1 teaspoon garam masala
• 2 teaspoons ground coriander
• 1 teaspoon ground cumin
• 1/2 teaspoon ground turmeric
• 1/2 teaspoon chili powder

- 1/4 teaspoon ground ginger
- 1/4 teaspoon ground cinnamon
- 1/2 teaspoon salt
- 1/2 cup chicken broth
- 1/4 cup dried fenugreek leaves

Instructions:
1. Heat the oil in a large skillet over medium heat. Add the onion and garlic and sauté until the onion is softened, about 5 minutes.
2. Add the garam masala, coriander, cumin, turmeric, chili powder, ginger, cinnamon, and salt. Stir until fragrant, about 1 minute.
3. Add the chicken and sauté until lightly golden, about 10 minutes.
4. Add the chicken broth and cover the skillet. Simmer for 20 minutes.
5. Add the fenugreek leaves and stir until combined. Simmer until the chicken is cooked through, about 10 minutes.

Nutrition information:
Calories: 288, Fat: 13 g, Carbohydrates: 7 g, Protein: 34 g, Sodium: 433 mg, Fiber: 3 g

77. Lahori Khoya Kulfi

Lahori Khoya Kulfi is a traditional Indian sweet dish made with condensed milk, cardamom and freshly made khoya.
Serving: 6
Preparation Time: 10 minutes
Ready Time: 2 to 4 hours

Ingredients:
- 2 liters full fat milk
- 1 cup freshly prepared khoya
- ¼ cup sugar
- 10-12 cardamom pods
- Some rose water
- 2 tablespoons sliced almonds

Instructions:

1. Boil the milk in a large pot over medium heat and cook until it has reduced to half its original volume.
2. Then, add the freshly prepared khoya and cook for about 5 minutes.
3. Add sugar and cardamom pods and cook for a few more minutes until the mixture thickens.
4. Then, remove from heat and let it cool down completely.
5. Once cooled, transfer the mixture to a shallow, freezer-safe container and sprinkle the sliced almonds.
6. Cover the container and place it in the freezer.
7. Let the mixture freeze for at least 2 to 4 hours.
8. Before serving, add a few drops of rose water and enjoy!

Nutrition information: (per serving)
Calories: 95 kcal, Carbohydrates: 9.4 g, Fat: 4.6 g, Protein: 3.3 g, Sodium: 51 mg, Sugar: 8.3 g

78. Lahori Tandoori Roti

Lahori tandoori roti is an incredibly flavourful and nutrient-rich flatbread made with whole wheat flour. It has a texture that is slightly chewy and fluffy, making it a favourite among foodies.
Serving: 4
Preparation time: 15 minutes
Ready time: 45 minutes

Ingredients:
- 2 cups whole wheat flour
- 1 teaspoon cumin seeds
- 1 teaspoon coriander seeds
- 2 tablespoons oil
- 2 tablespoons ghee
- 1/2 teaspoon salt
- Water, as required

Instructions:
1. In a large bowl, mix together the wheat flour, cumin seeds, coriander seeds, oil, ghee and salt.
2. Slowly add water and knead the dough until it is soft and pliable.

3. Cover the dough and let it rest for 15 minutes.
4. Divide the dough into 8 equal portions and roll out each portion into a 6-7 inch circle.
5. Pre-heat a fan grill or an oven to the highest temperature.
6. Place the rotis on the hot griddle and let it cook until spots start to appear.
7. Flip the roti over and cook the other side until golden brown spots appear.
8. Repeat with the remaining dough.
9. Serve the tandoori rotis hot.

Nutrition information:
- Calories:138 Kcal
- Protein:3 g
- Fat:6 g
- Carbohydrates: 18 g

79. Lahori Chana Pulao

Lahori Chana Pulao is one of the most popular Pakistani recipes made with Chickpeas and Rice. This dish has a spicy and flavoursome taste which is sure to tingle your taste buds.
Serving - 4
Preparation Time - 15 minutes
Ready in - 30 minutes

Ingredients:
- 2 cups Basmati Rice
- 1 can Chickpeas
- 2 tablespoons vegetable oil
- 2 cloves garlic - minced
- 2 medium onions - diced
- 2 teaspoons ground coriander
- 1 teaspoon ground cumin
- 1/2 teaspoon garam masala
- 1/2 teaspoon ground turmeric
- 2 cups chicken broth
- 1 tablespoon tomato paste

- Salt and pepper to taste
- 1/4 cup chopped cilantro

Instructions:
1. Rinse and drain the rice. Heat the vegetable oil in a large pot over medium heat. Add the garlic, onions, and spices and cook until fragrant, about 3 minutes.
2. Add the rice, stirring constantly to coat in the oil and spices for about 2 minutes. Add the chicken broth, chickpeas, and tomato paste and stir to combine.
3. Reduce heat to low and simmer for about 15 minutes, or until the rice is tender.
4. Season with salt and pepper to taste, and garnish with chopped cilantro. Serve hot.

Nutrition information -Per Serving -Calories: 403, Total Fat: 11 g, Saturated Fat: 2 g, Cholesterol: 0 mg, Sodium: 125 mg, Carbohydrates: 56 g, Protein: 14 g, Fiber: 6 g

80. Lahori Chicken Hariyali Tikka

Lahori Chicken Hariyali Tikka is a delicious and flavorful dish adapted from Pakistani Street food. It consists of marinated chicken, which is cooked over charcoal to bring out its smoky flavor. This dish is sure to not only tantalize your taste buds, but also bring variety to your meal.
Serving: 4
Preparation Time: 20 minutes
Ready Time: 40 minutes

Ingredients:
- 1kg (2 lbs) chicken, cut into cubes
- 2 tablespoons mustard oil
- 1 onion, chopped
- 2 tablespoons garlic paste
- 2 tablespoons ginger paste
- 2 tablespoons chilli paste
- 2 tablespoons coriander powder
- 1 tablespoon garam masala

- 2 tablespoons lemon juice
- 2 tablespoons freshly chopped coriander leaves
- Salt, to taste

Instructions:
1. Marinate the chicken cubes with salt, mustard oil, garlic paste, ginger paste, chilli paste, coriander powder and garam masala for around 15 minutes.
2. Heat the oil in a pan and add the chopped onion. Fry for 2 minutes on medium heat.
3. Add the marinated chicken cubes and fry the mixture for 5–10 minutes or until the chicken is cooked through.
4. Add the lemon juice and freshly chopped coriander leaves and stir for 3 minutes.
5. Serve the Lahori Chicken Hariyali Tikka hot with mashed potatoes and garlic naan or chapati.

Nutrition information: Calories - 268 Kcal, Total Fat - 14.5g, Cholesterol - 97.4 g, Sodium - 784.6mg, Potassium - 537.1mg, Total Carbs - 7.4g, Dietary Fiber - 0.8g, Sugars - 1.1g, Protein - 26.3g

81. Lahori Gola Kabab

Lahori Gola Kabab is a scrumptious and popular dish in Pakistan. It usually includes Chicken, Hara Bhara Kabab flavored with ginger, garlic, spices & herbs.
Serving: 4 people
Preparation time: 45 minutes
Ready time: 1 hour

Ingredients:
- 1 kg boneless chicken, cut into cubes
- 4 tbsp charmagaz, ground
- 1 tsp coriander powder
- 2 tsp kitchen king masala
- 2 tbsp garlic paste
- 1 tsp red chilli powder
- 2 tbsp ginger paste

- 2 tbsp lemon juice
- 2 beaten eggs
- Breadcrumbs
- Salt to taste
- Oil for shallow fry

Instructions:
1. Take the chicken cubes and add all the dry spices including charmagaz, coriander powder, kitchen king masala, red chilli powder, salt, and lemon juice. Mix all the Ingredients together.
2. In another bowl mix together garlic paste, ginger paste and eggs, then add it to the chicken mix and make sure to blend all the Ingredients together.
3. Then, make equal-sized balls out of the mixture and roll them in breadcrumbs.
4. Heat oil in a pan and shallow fry the chicken balls until golden brown and cooked through.
5. Serve hot with chutney and salads.

Nutrition information:
Serving Size: 1 kabab
Calories: 176.7
Total Fat: 15.9 g
Saturated Fat: 2.1 g
Polyunsaturated Fat: 4.9 g
Monounsaturated Fat: 6.8 g
Cholesterol: 43.2 mg
Sodium: 97.1 mg
Potassium: 178.2 mg
Total Carbohydrate: 1.7 g
Dietary Fiber: 0.5 g
Sugars: 0.3 g
Protein: 8.9 g

82. Lahori Chicken Pakora

Lahori Chicken Pakora is a popular snack in the Lahore region of Pakistan. It is made with chicken, spices, and a deep-frying technique, creating a flavorful, crunchy snack.

Serving: 6

Preparation time: 25 minutes

Ready time: 35 minutes

Ingredients:

-1 lb boneless, skinless chicken breasts, cut into chunks
-1 cup all-purpose flour
-1/2 cup chickpea flour
-1 teaspoon coriander powder
-1/2 teaspoon cumin powder
-1/4 teaspoon chili powder
-1 teaspoon garlic paste
-1 teaspoon ginger paste
-1/2 teaspoon turmeric powder
-Salt, to taste
-1/2 cup water
-Vegetable oil, for frying

Instructions:

1. In a large bowl, combine the chicken, all-purpose flour, chickpea flour, coriander, cumin, chili powder, garlic paste, ginger paste, turmeric, and salt. Mix together until everything is well combined.
2. Slowly add the water and mix until a thick batter is formed.
3. In a large deep pot, heat vegetable oil on medium-high heat.
4. Using your hands, take a small amount of the batter and shape into a round pakora shape. Carefully lower it into the oil and repeat with the remaining batter.
5. Fry the pakoras until golden-brown and crispy. Remove from the oil and place onto a paper towel-lined plate to drain.

Nutrition information:

Per Serving:

Calories: 325

Fat: 15g

Carbohydrates: 27g

Protein: 19g

83. Lahori Baingan Ka Raita

Lahori Baingan Ka Raita is a popular Punjabi dish which is a mouth-watering combination of eggplant, yogurt, and spices. This tasty dish is a great accompaniment for roti or paratha.

Serving: 4
Preparation time: 15 minutes
Ready time: 30 minutes

Ingredients:
- 2 large eggplants
- 2 green chillies
- 1/2 tsp cumin seeds
- 3 tbsp oil
- 1 tomato, finely chopped
- 1/2 tsp smoked red chilli powder
- 1/2 tsp turmeric powder
- 2 cup plain yogurt
- 1/2 tsp garam masala
- Salt to taste
- Chopped coriander leaves for garnishing

Instructions:
1. Preheat the oven to 375°F. Place the eggplants on a baking tray lined with parchment paper and bake them for 25-30 minutes or until soft.
2. Once the eggplants are cooked, remove them from the oven and make a slit in the eggplant. Scoop out the soft flesh, discard the skins and mash the flesh.
3. Heat oil in a pan and add the cumin seeds. Once the seeds start spluttering, add the green chillies and tomato. Cook for a few minutes and then add the mashed eggplant.
4. Add the smoked red chilli powder, turmeric powder, garam masala and salt and cook for 10 minutes.
5. Now add the yogurt and mix everything thoroughly. Simmer for 5-10 minutes until the raita is cooked.
6. Garnish with chopped coriander leaves.

Nutrition information:

Calories - 213 kcal
Fat - 13.2 g
Carbohydrates - 16.7 g
Protein - 8.5 g
Fiber - 4.5 g

84. Lahori Mutton Chops

Lahori Mutton Chops is a popular Pakistani specialty with succulent pieces of juicy mutton ribs that are slathered in a mix of spices and cooked to perfection!
Serving: 8
Preparation Time: 15 minutes
Ready Time: 2 hours

Ingredients:
• 3 kg mutton ribs, chopped
• 2 large onions, finely chopped
• 2 -3 tablespoons garlic paste
• 2 -3 tablespoons ginger paste
• ¼ cup freshly squeezed lemon juice
• 2 tablespoons red chili powder
• 1 teaspoon garam masala
• 1 teaspoon cumin powder
• 2 tablespoons vegetable oil
• 1 tablespoon mustard powder
• Salt to taste
• Fresh cilantro leaves for garnishing

Instructions:
1. In a large bowl, add the mutton ribs, onion, garlic and ginger pastes, lemon juice, red chili powder, garam masala, cumin powder, vegetable oil, mustard powder, and salt and mix until well combined.
2. Heat a large skillet over medium heat and add the mutton mixture. Cook for 15-20 minutes, stirring occasionally, until the mutton is cooked through and the sauce has reduced and thickened.
3. Transfer the cooked mutton to a platter and garnish with cilantro leaves. Serve hot with naan or roti.

Nutrition information:
Calories: 477 kcal, Carbs: 4g, Protein: 75g, Fat: 13g, Cholesterol: 177 mg, Sodium: 275 mg, Sugar: 0.6 g, Fiber: 1.3 g.

85. Lahori Aloo Methi

Lahori Aloo Methi is a delicious traditional Pakistani dish that combines potatoes, fenugreek leaves, and spices to create a wonderful combination of flavors and textures. With its robust flavors, this dish is sure to win the hearts of everyone around the dinner table.
Serving: 6
Preparation time: 15 minutes
Ready time: 45 minutes

Ingredients:
3 tablespoons vegetable oil
1/2 teaspoon cumin seeds
1/2 teaspoon cardamom seeds
1 onion, chopped
3 cloves garlic, minced
1 tablespoon fresh ginger, grated
2 green chillies, chopped
3 potatoes, cubed
1 teaspoon ground turmeric
2 tablespoons coriander powder
1 teaspoon garam masala
1 teaspoon amchur, (optional)
2 cups chopped fresh fenugreek leaves
1 teaspoon dried fenugreek leaves
Salt to taste

Instructions:
1. Heat the oil in a large pan over medium-high heat.
2. Add the cumin and cardamom seeds and fry for about 30 seconds.
3. Add the onion, garlic, and ginger and fry until the onion is translucent.
4. Add the potatoes and fry for 5-7 minutes, stirring frequently.

5. Add the turmeric, coriander powder, garam masala, amchur (if using), and salt and mix well.
6. Add the fresh and dried fenugreek leaves and mix well.
7. Reduce heat to medium-low and simmer for 20-25 minutes, stirring occasionally.
8. Serve hot with chapatis or steamed rice.

Nutrition information:
Calories: 219
Protein: 6g
Carbohydrates: 23g
Fat: 13g
Fiber: 5g
Sodium: 221mg

86. Lahori Chicken Keema Paratha

Lahori Chicken Keema Paratha is a savory dish of Pakistani origin. It is made by stuffing a paratha dough with a tangy and spicy ground chicken keema. The dish is served hot with mint or tamarind chutney.
Serving: 4 - 6
Preparation Time: 10 minutes
Ready Time: 40 minutes

Ingredients:
- 2 cups all-purpose flour
- 1/2 teaspoon salt
- 1/2 teaspoon oil
- 1/2 teaspoon red chili powder
- 1/2 teaspoon ground cumin
- 3 tablespoons coriander powder
- 1/2 teaspoon garam masala
- 2 green chilies, chopped
- 1 onion, chopped
- 2 cups ground chicken keema
- 1/4 cup chopped fresh coriander leaves
- Salt to taste
- Oil, for shallow-frying

Instructions:

1. In a large bowl, mix the all-purpose flour, salt, oil, red chili powder, ground cumin, coriander powder, and garam masala. Make a well in the center and add 1/2 cup of warm water. Knead to make a soft dough. Cover with a damp cloth and set aside for 15 minutes.

2. Meanwhile, in a skillet, heat some oil over medium heat. Add the green chilies and onion and sauté for 3 - 4 minutes or until the onion turns golden brown.

3. Add the ground chicken keema, coriander leaves, and salt to the pan and cook for 5 - 6 minutes or until the chicken is cooked through. Set aside to cool.

4. Divide the dough into 4 - 6 portions. Take one portion of the dough and roll it out into a circle of 4 inches (about 10 cm) in diameter.

5. Place 1 tablespoon of the cooled chicken keema mixture into the center of the circle.

6. Bring up the edges of the circle and pinch together to seal the keema mixture in the center.

7. Flatten the stuffed dough, roll it out again into a thin circle and prick it with a fork.

8. Heat a griddle over medium heat. Place the paratha on the griddle and shallow fry it until lightly browned on both sides, adding a few tablespoons of oil if needed.

Nutrition information: (Per Serving)

Calories: 287
Carbohydrates: 28g
Protein: 20g
Fat: 10g
Saturated fat: 2g
Cholesterol: 49mg
Sodium: 522mg
Potassium: 257mg

87. Lahori Mix Sabzi

Lahori Mix Sabzi is a unique and flavorful vegetable dish. This traditional Punjabi dish features a blend of fresh vegetables and herbs cooked in oil, traditional spices, and tangy tomato paste. It's best served hot with naan, roti, or other flatbread.

Serving: Serves 4
Preparation Time: 25 minutes
Ready Time: 45 minutes

Ingredients:
- 2 tablespoons oil
- 2 large onions, chopped
- 1 teaspoon ginger garlic paste
- 2 medium tomatoes, chopped
- 1 cup cauliflower florets
- 2/3 cup green beans, cut into 1-inch pieces
- 2 potatoes, cubed
- 2 carrots, chopped
- 1 teaspoon cumin seeds
- 1 teaspoon red chili powder
- 1/2 teaspoon turmeric powder
- Salt, to taste
- 2 tablespoons tomato paste
- 2 tablespoons chopped cilantro
- 1/2 cup frozen peas, thawed

Instructions:
1. Heat the oil in a large skillet over medium-high heat.
add the onions and sauté until they are golden brown.
2. Add the ginger garlic paste and sauté for 1 minute.
3. Add the tomatoes and cook until they become soft.
4. Add the cauliflower, green beans, potatoes, and carrots to the skillet.
5. Add the cumin, red chili powder, turmeric, salt, and tomato paste. Mix well and cook for 10 minutes, stirring occasionally.
6. Add the cilantro and peas and stir to combine. Simmer for 5 minutes.
7. Serve hot with naan, roti, or other flatbread.

Nutrition information:
Calories - 145 kcal, Total Fat - 5 g, Cholesterol - 0 g, Carbohydrates - 21 g, Protein - 4 g, Sodium - 103 mg, Fiber - 6 g

88. Lahori Mutton Rogan Josh

Lahori Mutton Rogan Josh is an aromatic and delicious curry dish from the region of Lahore in Pakistan. It is widely enjoyed around the world by many cultures and is deliciously savory and hearty.
Serving: Serves 4
Preparation Time: 10 minutes
Ready Time: 45 minutes

Ingredients:
-1.5kg Mutton, cubed
-4 tablespoons ghee
-4 cardamom pods
-3 cloves
-2 bay leaves
-1 teaspoon cumin seeds
-2 teaspoon black peppercorns
-2 teaspoons red chilli powder
-1 teaspoon coriander powder
-1 teaspoon turmeric powder
-2 cups yoghurt, whisked
-4 tablespoons Kashmiri red chilli powder
-1 tablespoon garam masala
-1 teaspoon ginger paste
-1 teaspoon garlic paste
-1 teaspoon salt
-1 cup water
-2 tablespoons chopped fresh coriander

Instructions:
1. Heat ghee in a large pot over a medium heat. Add the cardamom pods, cloves, bay leaves, cumin seeds, and black peppercorns and sauté for 2 minutes, stirring constantly.
2. Add the mutton to the pot and stir to mix in the spices. Cook for about 10 minutes, stirring occasionally.
3. Add the red chilli powder, coriander powder, and turmeric powder to the pot and stir until combined.
4. Layer the whisked yoghurt and Kashmiri red chilli powder over the mutton and stir to combine.

5. Add the garam masala, ginger paste, garlic paste, and salt to the pot and stir to combine.
6. Add the water to the pot and stir. Bring the mixture to a boil.
7. Lower the heat and cover the pot with a lid. Simmer the curry for 25 minutes, stirring occasionally.
8. Uncover the pot and cook for an additional 10 minutes until the sauce has thickened.
9. Turn off the heat and sprinkle the chopped fresh coriander over the curry.

Nutrition information: Per serve: 582 kcal; 24.2g fat; 6.2g saturated fat; 37.7g protein; 3.5g carbohydrate; 1.5g sugar; 4.7g fiber

89. Lahori Matar Pulao

Lahori Matar Pulao is a perfect combination of rice and peas and is a popular dish from Pakistan. The spices used to make this dish highlight the amazing flavor.
Serving: 4
Preparation Time: 20 minutes
Ready Time: 30 minutes

Ingredients:
- 2 tablespoons oil
- 1 teaspoon cumin seeds
- 1/2 teaspoon garlic paste
- 2 cups basmati rice
- 1 cup peas
- 2 cups water
- 1/2 teaspoon salt
- 1/2 teaspoon red chilli powder
- 1/2 teaspoon coriander powder
- 1/4 teaspoon garam masala
- 1/4 teaspoon turmeric powder

Instructions:
1. Heat oil in a pressure cooker and add cumin seeds.
2. Once the seeds start to crackle, add garlic paste and fry for 30 seconds.

3. Now add the basmati rice, peas, water and all the spices.
4. Give it a good stir and cover the lid. Cook for 4-5 whistles.
5. Once the pressure is released, open the lid and fluff the rice with a fork.

Nutrition information:
Calories per Serving: 223
Total Fat: 6 Iron: 1.3
Total Carbohydrates: 38.5
Protein: 5.8
Sodium: 337 mg
Cholesterol: 0 mg

90. Lahori Chicken Bharta

Lahori Chicken Bharta is a traditional Pakistani dish that consists of minced chicken combined with spicy, aromatic Ingredients. This dish is simmered with garlic, ginger, and other spices, resulting in a flavorful and tantalizing flavor.
Serving: 4
Preparation Time: 15 minutes
Ready Time: 45 minutes

Ingredients:
• 2 tablespoons vegetable oil
• 2 cloves garlic, minced
• 2 tablespoons minced ginger
• 1 teaspoon cumin
• 1 teaspoon coriander
• 1 teaspoon Kashmiri red chili powder
• 2 cups chicken, minced
• 1 onion, chopped
• 1 tomato, chopped
• 1/2 cup yogurt
• 1/2 teaspoon garam masala
• 1/2 teaspoon sugar
• Salt, to taste
• 2 tablespoons cilantro, chopped

Instructions:
1. Heat the oil in a large skillet over medium heat.
2. Add the garlic and ginger and cook for about 2 minutes.
3. Add the cumin, coriander and Kashmiri red chili powder, and cook for 1 minute.
4. Add the minced chicken and cook, stirring often, until the chicken is cooked through.
5. Add the onion, tomato, yogurt, garam masala and sugar and bring to a boil.
6. Reduce the heat to low and simmer for 25 minutes, stirring occasionally.
7. Add salt to taste and simmer for an additional 10 minutes.
8. Serve with chopped cilantro.

Nutrition information:
Serving Size: 1 cup
Calories: 200
Fat: 9g
Protein: 14g
Carbohydrates: 12g
Sugars: 4g
Fiber: 2g
Sodium: 75 mg

91. Lahori Kachumber Salad

Lahori Kachumber Salad is a traditional Pakistani style salad. It's a delightful mix of crisp vegetables and tangy flavors that will tantalize your taste buds! It is light and very easy to make.
Serving: 4
Preparation Time: 10 minutes
Ready Time: 10 minutes

Ingredients:
- 2 Tomatoes, diced
- 1 Cucumber, diced
- 1 Onion, sliced

- 2 Green chilies, diced
- 1/4 cup Fresh cilantro, chopped
- 2 tablespoons Lemon juice
- 1 teaspoon Chaat masala
- Salt, to taste

Instructions:
1. In a large bowl, combine the tomatoes, cucumber, onion, green chilies, cilantro, lemon juice, chaat masala and salt.
2. Mix well and taste for seasoning. Adjust, if needed.
3. Serve chilled or at room temperature.

Nutrition information:
Calories: 40, Total Fat: 0 g, Saturated Fat: 0 g, Trans Fat: 0 g, Cholesterol: 0 mg, Sodium: 120 mg, Total Carbohydrate: 8 g, Dietary Fiber: 2 g, Sugar: 3 g, Protein: 1 g

92. Lahori Chicken Chapli Kebab

Lahori Chicken Chapli Kebab is a delicious Pakistani fried patty made with ground chicken, turmeric, cumin and a variety of other spices. It is a popular dish for parties and gatherings.
Serving: 4-5 people
Preparation Time: 15 minutes
Ready Time: 45 minutes

Ingredients:
1 lb ground chicken
1 teaspoon turmeric
2 tablespoon cumin
1 teaspoon black pepper
1 teaspoon red chilli powder
1/2 teaspoon coriander powder
1/4 teaspoon garam masala powder
2 teaspoon ginger paste
2 teaspoon garlic paste
2 tablespoon plain yoghurt
2 tablespoon oil

Salt to taste

Instructions:
1. In a large bowl, mix together the chicken, turmeric, cumin, pepper, chilli powder, coriander powder, garam masala, ginger paste, garlic paste, yoghurt and 2 tablespoon oil.
2. Season with salt to taste and combine the Ingredients well.
3. Form the mixture into 10 even sized patties.
4. Heat the remaining oil in a large skillet over medium-high heat and place the patties in the skillet.
5. Fry the patties on both sides until deep golden and crisp.
6. Serve the Lahori Chicken Chapli Kebab hot.

Nutrition information:
Calories: 235 kcal
Fat: 17 g
Carbohydrates: 2 g
Protein: 19 g
Sodium: 137 mg

93. Lahori Dahi Bhalla

Lahori Dahi Bhalla is a Pakistani delicacy whose unique flavor is unmatchable. This dish is made with round, deep-fried chickpea flour balls that are usually slow-cooked in dahi (yogurt) and spices.
Serving: 4 people
Preparation Time: 10 minutes
Ready Time: 30 minutes

Ingredients:
• 1 cup yogurt
• 2 cups water
• 2 tbsp chickpea flour
• 2 green chilies
• 1 tsp red chili powder
• 1 tsp salt
• 2 tsp cumin powder
• 2 tsp chaat masala

- 2 tsp roasted cumin powder
- 2 tbsp chopped green coriander
- 4 tbsp cooking oil
- 4 tbsp tamarind chutney

Instructions:

1. In a bowl, whisk together the yogurt, water, chickpea flour, green chilies, red chili powder, salt, cumin powder, and chaat masala.
2. Heat the oil in a deep frying pan.
3. Drop spoonfuls of the chickpea batter into the hot oil and fry until golden.
4. Using a slotted spoon, remove the fried bhallay from the oil and set aside.
5. In a large bowl, combine the yogurt mixture, roasted cumin powder, chopped green coriander, and tamarind chutney.
6. Add the bhallay to the mixture.
7. Mix everything together, ensuring that the bhallay are completely coated in the yogurt.
8. Garnish with chopped green coriander and serve.

Nutrition information: per Serving
- Calories: 149 Kcal
- Carbohydrates: 15.5 g
- Protein: 5.8 g
- Fat: 8.4 g
- Cholesterol: 4 mg

94. Lahori Baingan Raita

Lahori Baingan Raita is a creamy, spicy, and flavorful dish made with mashed eggplants and yogurt. It originates from Lahore, a city in Pakistan.
Serving: 4
Preparation Time: 10 minutes
Ready Time: 25 minutes

Ingredients:
- 3 medium eggplants

- 2-3 cups of plain yogurt
- 4 tablespoons of vegetable oil
- 2 onions, chopped
- 2 cloves of garlic, minced
- 1 teaspoon of ground cumin
- 1 teaspoon of ground coriander
- ½ teaspoon of ground turmeric
- 2 teaspoons of sea salt
- 1 teaspoon of red chilli powder
- 2 tablespoons of fresh cilantro, chopped
- 2 tablespoons of fresh mint

Instructions:
1. Preheat oven to 375 degrees F.
2. Arrange the eggplants on a baking sheet lined with parchment paper. Bake for 25 minutes or until eggplant is soft and cooked through.
3. Remove eggplants from the oven and let them cool.
4. Mash the eggplants with a fork or potato masher.
5. In a large bowl, combine together the mashed eggplants, yogurt, oil, onions, garlic, cumin, coriander, turmeric, sea salt, red chilli powder, cilantro and mint. Mix together well.
6. Serve the Lahori Baingan Raita chilled or at room temperature.

Nutrition information: Per serving: 121 calories, 8g fat, 2g saturated fat, 10g carbohydrates, 3g protein, 340mg sodium, 2g fiber.

95. Lahori Mutton Haleem

Lahori Mutton Haleem is a flavorful, comforting dish from the Pakistani province of Punjab. It is made of a mixture of wheat, lentils, barley, and meat, cooked together until the dish has reached a thick consistency. It is traditionally served as comfort food in the cold winter months, but is enjoyed all year round.
Serving: 4
Preparation Time: 30 minutes
Ready Time: 2-3 hours

Ingredients:

- 1 lb. mutton, cut into small pieces
- 1/2 cup split red lentils
- 1/4 cup whole wheat
- 1/4 cup barley
- 4-5 cloves
- 2 black cardamoms
- 8-10 chilies
- 1/2 tsp. garlic paste
- 2-3 tsp. ginger paste
- salt to taste
- 2-3 tbsp. clarified butter

Instructions:
1. Soak the lentils, wheat, and barley overnight.
2. In a large pot, add the mutton and soaked lentils, wheat, and barley.
3. Add enough water to cover everything in the pot.
4. Add the cloves, cardamoms, chilies, garlic paste, ginger paste, and salt.
5. Simmer on low heat for 2-3 hours, stirring occasionally, until the mutton and lentils are cooked through.
6. Remove from the heat and add the clarified butter.
7. Puree the Ingredients until a thick, paste-like consistency is reached.
8. Transfer into a serving dish and serve with naan or chapati.

Nutrition information: Nutrition per Serving: Calories: 303, Fat: 5g, Carbs: 40g, Protein: 21g, Sodium: 250mg

96. Lahori Matar Paneer

Lahori Matar Paneer is a flavorful, vegan-friendly curry from the region of Lahore, Pakistan. It is irresistibly creamy and rich in spices, and makes a delightful addition to any meal.
Serving: 4
Preparation Time: 10 minutes
Ready Time: 20 minutes

Ingredients:
- 2 tablespoons of vegetable oil
- 1 teaspoon of cumin seeds

- 1 large onion, minced
- 1 teaspoon of garam masala
- 1 teaspoon of ground coriander
- ¼ teaspoon of ground turmeric
- 2 garlic cloves, minced
- 1 (28-ounce) can crushed tomatoes
- 1 cup of frozen peas
- 1 (14-ounce) can full-fat coconut milk
- 1 (14-ounce) can of paneer cubes
- Fresh cilantro leaves, for garnish

Instructions:
1. Heat the oil in a large skillet over medium heat. Add the cumin seeds and cook for 1 minute, stirring constantly.
2. Add the onion and sauté for 2-3 minutes, until softened and translucent. Stir in the garam masala, ground coriander, and turmeric. Continue to cook for 1 minute.
3. Add the garlic and cook for 1 minute.
4. Add the crushed tomatoes and peas and bring to a simmer. Simmer for 10 minutes, stirring occasionally.
5. Add the coconut milk and paneer cubes and stir to combine. Simmer over low heat for 10 minutes, stirring occasionally.
6. Serve the Lahori Matar Paneer with fresh cilantro, if desired.

Nutrition information:
Calories: 434 kcal, Carbohydrates: 28g, Protein: 16g, Fat: 29g, Saturated Fat: 19g, Cholesterol: 28mg, Sodium: 294mg, Potassium: 533mg, Fiber: 5g, Sugar: 8g, Vitamin A: 771IU, Vitamin C: 35mg, Calcium: 238mg, Iron: 4mg.

97. Lahori Keema Karela

Lahori Keema Karela is a scrumptiously flavorful and delightful Pakistani dish made of minced meat and bitter gourd.
Serving: 4
Preparation Time: 15 minutes
Ready Time: 30 minutes

Ingredients:
1 lb. ground beef
1 lb. karela (otherwise known as bitter gourd)
1 large onion, minced
1 teaspoon cumin
1 teaspoon hot paprika
1 teaspoon ginger powder
1 teaspoon turmeric
1 teaspoon garlic powder
2 tablespoons tomato paste
Salt to taste

Instructions:
1. Start by cutting the karela into slices about 1/4 inch thick.
2. In a large skillet, heat about two tablespoons of oil over medium heat.
3. Add the minced onion and sauté for two to three minutes, until the onion starts to soften.
4. Add the ground beef and cook for another four to five minutes, until it is fully cooked.
5. Add the karela slices and stir to combine.
6. Add the cumin, hot paprika, ginger powder, turmeric, garlic powder, tomato paste, and salt.
7. Cook for another four to five minutes, until the karela is softened.
8. Serve the Lahori Keema Karela warm and enjoy!

Nutrition information:
Calories: 280
Total Fat: 12g
Carbohydrates: 16g
Protein: 24g
Sugars: 7g
Sodium: 85mg

98. Lahori Gajrela

Lahori Gajrela is a classic Pakistani dessert made of grated carrots cooked in thick milk, sugar, whole spices, ghee, and nuts. It is a delicious sweet dish that can be served after meals or as a dessert.

Serving: 8
Preparation time: 15 minutes
Ready time: 45 minutes

Ingredients:
-1 kilogram grated carrots
-1 litre full-fat milk
-100g sugar
-2 tablespoons ghee
-Green cardamom
-Pistachios
-Almonds

Instructions:
1. Heat ghee in a large pan, add grated carrots and fry for 4-5 minutes on medium heat.
2. Pour milk over it and mix. Cook until the milk reduces to half.
3. Add sugar and mix. Cook until the carrots are cooked and the mixture thickens.
4. Add green cardamom, pistachios, and almonds. Stir and cook for 2-3 more minutes.
5. Turn off the heat and serve Lahori Gajrela warm.

Nutrition information: Per serving (240g) of Lahori Gajrela provides around 360 calories, 15g fat, 47g carbohydrates, 6g protein, and 8g fiber.

CONCLUSION

This cookbook, Flavors of Lahore: A Collection of 98 Traditional Recipes, has been a welcome addition to any kitchen. For those unfamiliar with Pakistani cuisine, it offers a fantastic introduction, while for those with an established knowledge of the genre, this cookbook provides an invaluable vessel to explore more fully the culinary nuances of Lahore and the Punjab region.

Throughout these 98 recipes, the reader is taken on a sumptuous journey that highlights the vibrant flavors of Lahore. From Punjabi classics like Kiblahi, Butter Chicken, and Sai Bahaar, to modern flavor twists such as Baked Bitter Melon and Sweet Corn Cake, this book offers something for everyone. Additionally, the beautifully written stories and anecdotes included throughout the book provide meaningful insight into the culture and history of Lahore.

The recipes featured in Flavors of Lahore are easily adaptable to all diets, and no matter where one is located, all that is required are ingredients that are readily available in most global supermarkets. Also, the beauty of these recipes is that they can be adapted to the preferences of the individual cook, providing a customizable and enjoyable experience in the kitchen.

Flavors of Lahore is not just a cookbook; it is an ingredient-based exploration into the depths of Lahore's food culture. From the inspirations to the rituals, this book provides an immersive and enriching experience. Each time the reader flips through the pages of Flavors of Lahore, there is an opportunity to learn, grow, and explore.

As the stories, recipes, and flavors within this cookbook suggest, Lahore is home to a culture that is centred around the plate. It is a city of wonders that provides us with a vast palette of flavors and textures that tantalize the palate and bring people together. The recipes in Flavors of Lahore capture and embody the flavor and spirit of Lahore, allowing us to bring a little piece of the city with us wherever we go.

Made in United States
North Haven, CT
28 January 2024

48045019R00065